Walk-ins Among Us

Open Your Personal Portal to Cosmic Awareness

Yvonne Perry

Write On! Publishing
Nashville, Tennessee

Acknowledgments

Whenever I write a book, I have to "test drive" or validate its content. This usually means I encounter something within myself that must be cleared in order to become more fully empowered and live the message I'm sharing with my readers. I am especially thankful to those who helped me through the rough places in birthing *Walk-ins Among Us*: Randy Perry, Maxine Taylor, Brenda Williams, Dr. Tom Goode, Dr. Caron Goode, and Carl Bozeman.

Maxine Taylor, you helped me more than words can express. Thank you for helping me to release my childhood story and move into the magic.

Thank you, Brenda Williams, for teaching me the Reset Breath© and Quiet Touch© and helping me understand what it means to hold a personal field of eighteen inches.

Thank you, Dana Micheli, for the copy edit on the book.

Thank you, Rick Chappell, for the wonderful art design and layout for the cover of this book.

Contents

Noted author Yvonne Perry has another winner, an excellent well-written book called *Walk-ins Among Us* in the paranormal genre. The title echoes in the ears of those who read the popular metaphysical book called *Strangers Among Us* by author Ruth Montgomery in the late 1970s. Exceeding Montgomery's prose, Yvonne deftly blends the the explanations of how the walk-in experience unfolds, and clarifies the united viewpoint of those who have walked-in, and reports why more of these experiences may continue. You'll enjoy Yvonne's straightforward approach, written with the authority of an investigative journalist and her transparency, shared from an open heart.

Dr. Caron Goode, author International Bestseller of *Kids Who See Ghosts, Guide Them through Fear*

Other Books by Yvonne Perry

Shifting into Purer Consciousness ~ Integrating Spiritual Transformation with the Human Experience (http://shiftingintopurerconsciousness.com)

Whose Stuff Is This? Finding Freedom from the Thoughts, Feelings, and Energy of Those Around You (http://WhoseStuffIsThis.com)

More Than Meets the Eye, True Stories about Death, Dying, and Afterlife (http://deathdyingafterlife.com)

The Sid Series ~ A Collection of Holistic Stories for Children (http://TheSidSeries.com)

Foreword

When I first learned about walk-ins back in the early 1980s, I was absolutely fascinated, and could not learn enough about them. Unfortunately, there was not a great deal of information available on walk-ins at that time.

Over the years, I was fortunate enough to meet several and become friends with them. I interviewed them on my radio show, and felt drawn to the walk-in community. In my astrological practice, whenever I discovered that one of my clients was a walk-in, I did a special chart on them for the moment of their walk-in. (Walk-ins have two natal charts: the one for the walk-out and the one for the walk-in.) They are my favorite clients because they know they have a mission here on earth, and want to get on with it. We speak the same language.

When Yvonne told me that she was writing a book about walk-ins, I could not wait to read it. *Walk-Ins Among Us,* is cutting edge, and answers so many questions. In it, Yvonne shares her own story and brings us up-to-date on the current walk-in experiences.

Whether you are a walk-in, a starseed, or a light worker, or whether you simply want to know more about them, this eye-opening book will give you insight into our galactic community. It may leave you wanting more!

Maxine Taylor,

Georgia's first licensed astrologer since 1968, Maxine is the co-founder of the Metropolitan Atlanta Astrological Society, the Atlanta Board of Astrology Examiners, and the Atlanta Institute of Metaphysics. She is also the author of Amazon best-sellers, *Move into the Magic, What Your Astrologer Never Mentioned,* and *Now That I've Cast It, What Do I Do with It?* www.maxinetaylor.com

Introduction

I began writing this walk-in book twice. In the process, I ended up with two other books: *Whose Stuff Is This? ~ Finding Freedom from the Thoughts, Feelings, and Energy of Those Around You* and *Shifting Into Purer Consciousness ~ Integrating Spiritual Transformation with the Human Experience.* Those books are serving the divine plan of love, and yet I knew all along that there was another book that needed to come forth. So, this time I have written the book that has been on my heart for almost a decade.

It seems that the time is perfect for this material to be shared because the number of people having sudden transformations and walk-in experiences is increasing daily, and these "new" souls need some basic understanding of the process in order to acclimate and get on with accomplishing the purpose for which they came to this planet.

The general consensus is that walk-in souls are evolved enough to have energy or information to share with an awakening consciousness; therefore, they can avoid the birth and childhood process. Walk-ins are not better than any other soul on Earth, so there is no need to get caught up in the drama of that idea. In fact, the life of a walk-in is difficult, and many times lonely, because there are not many people they can talk to about their experience.

This book provides the help you will need if you experience a significant spiritual transformation in which you suddenly change many aspects of your life. Trying to acclimate to the faster vibrational energy from your oversoul, soul group, or multidimensional aspect of yourself can be daunting. This book is intended to help you feel safe and get connected with other walk-ins.

Because we are all multidimensional beings, everyone here on Earth is from someplace else. We are all here to do something, regardless of how or when we came to be in a human body. This book will help lightworkers, healers, starseeds, and indigos discover their mission and move toward making it a reality.

Whenever I mention the word "walk-in" (which I do not do with just anyone), I get a mixed response. Some are fascinated by the concept, some think I am downright crazy, and others give me a dropped-jaw, deer-in-the-headlights look. When that happens, I know a light bulb has just gone on in their heads, and it has "Ah-HA!" written all over it.

Every person on Earth has a personal journey to follow through the process of ascension. Like other Lightworkers (Indigos and Starseeds), Walk-ins are path-cutters or way-showers who have agreed to incarnate in order to heal, clear and release cellular patterns recorded in human DNA and the planetary grid. Many of us feel like misfits because we have the ability to operate in the multi-dimensional reality of our upper chakras, whereas most residents of this plane are operating only in the lower three energy centers.

As forerunners of the oneness evolution, we see the cosmic picture and awaken others by leading the way—many times through mystical experiences. We tend to get "star-being syndrome" when we see the ideal of how humans are *supposed* to function and then feel frustrated when others are seemly hypnotized and stuck in their unenlightened programming. I remember being called a "trailblazer" in a prophecy given over me by Mickey Robinson in the late 1990s. Although I have always been ahead of the pack when it comes to spiritual phenomena, this prophecy makes more sense to me now than it did back then. It helps me understand why my gifts were rejected by the church and why I have had such a problem with authority figures all my life. I have always been a rebel when it comes to adhering to social norms and this is part of the dismantling of old structures that dictate how we sustain our existence, do intimate relationships, and interact globally. We are assisting the plan of oneness by allowing our bodies to receive subatomic biological changes that will move all of us into a silica- or crystal-based form known as the light body. This process has been occurring for quite some time but has recently sped up as we entered the Age of Aquarius.

We are experiencing a cosmic convergence of starseeds, celestial beings, and walk-ins now arriving on Earth to connect with those already in body, who have paved the way. These advanced visitors are our future selves from other universes and planes of existence. You could be one of them. It is best that you determine for yourself whether or not you have had a walk-in experience. I support you in discovering your own truth and not just believing what someone else says about you. The purpose of this book is to help walk-ins move past the adjustment period and step into service as the empowered being that they are.

With the full permission of Ranoli, the past president of Walk-in Evolution International (WE), I have used material in this book that she wrote and posted on the WE website (http://walkinevolution.com/) and blog we co-maintain: (http://walkinevolution.blogspot.com/). I invite you to visit these sites and to interact in the discussions on our Facebook page: http://www.facebook.com/WalkInEvolution.

Chapter 1 - Walk-ins Welcome

I chuckle whenever I see a sign that reads "Walk-ins Welcome." It is so nice of businesses to extend an invitation to the star beings who come to Earth in a less traditional manner. They must know that some souls skip the baby, toddler, and young teen years and take up residence in a mature human body. I am sure that is what the signs indicate, right?

Everyone likes the convenience of walking into a place and getting instant service. We have walk-in medical clinics and walk-in hair salons where we can obtain services without having to wait. We walk into a restaurant and a server takes our drink order. A few minutes later we are sipping our favorite beverage, and our food comes to the table soon after. In the ideal world, our meals are free; but for now, let's say the check comes without our having to remind the server to bring it or wait for him to return with our change or credit card. A friend of mine told me he walked past a paper that was still rolled up in the protective plastic bag and the words "Walk-In" caught his eye. It was an advertisement for walk-in tubs. Really? The water would spill out when you open the door! I am still waiting for my walk-in closet to start putting my clothes on hangers—but overall, Earth life as a walk-in soul is a grand experience.

Even though we do have spirit beings to assist us, souls walking into an adult body, with all its quirks, conditioning, and dysfunction, may not get a grand welcome from humans upon arrival—certainly not like a soul entering as a sweet little newborn. No baby showers, designer nurseries, or parents and grandparents oohing and cooing over us. Nope. Most of our friends and family do not even know we are here, much less that the soul they celebrated when this body was born has left the building.

Many times, the body that a starseed soul walks into has some type of disease, injury, or emotional imbalance. The natal or walk-out soul may have left behind a distressing life situation such as limiting beliefs about him/herself, unenlightened social conditioning, or some detrimental, or even abusive, behaviors in its muscular and cellular memory. Additionally, the walk-in soul may feel disoriented, confused, and confined as it acclimates to expressing itself in a human body. By the way, a starseed is a soul who originated off-planet in another dimension and then incarnated into human form on the Earth plane. An earthseed soul navigates through life using only the lower three chakras governing survival on the planet. A starseed functions through the upper and lower chakras and is able to access and bring multidimensional reality into its Earth life experience.

Whenever a new owner takes possession of a property, there is work to be done. The walls may need to be painted, the flooring may need to be replaced, or the bath or kitchen may need to be completely remodeled. It is often the same with a soul exchange. The incoming soul inherits the décor, trash, weeds, and mess of the former soul. It is the responsibility of the walk-in soul to resolve and transmute the outstanding issues of the walk-out soul before the new soul's mission can begin in full. It is not uncommon for the walk-in to "gut" the relationships that the first soul maintained. Within the first twelve hours of walking into this body in 1999, I left a 22-year marriage. I also left organized religion, changed jobs, moved to a new location, stopped playing piano (something I had loved all my life), and experienced a huge change in personality.

If you think you are a walk-in, chances are you can look back on your journey and see a time when you went through multiple and sudden changes that drastically shifted the direction of your life. You may have awakened from a coma and realized that you were not the same person you were when you "went to sleep." Perhaps a suicide attempt, surgery, a serious medical condition or injury, a near-death experience, or a dark night of the soul preceded these changes. These are common situations that a natal soul may set up as an exit point.

Even though things seem to shift very quickly after a walk-in occurs, there is likely a transition period during which the walk-out and walk-in souls temporarily swap places to help both souls get accustomed to their new places and roles. It reminds me of the "try it before you buy it" concept of an HGTV show called *Sleep on It*, in which the potential buyer spends one night in a house before making a decision about purchasing it. The natal soul of the body I now occupy contemplated divorce for several years, but was unable to take action. This urge to break up was likely part of the incoming soul's prep work. She knew that the walk-out's marriage would not serve her mission, and the first thing she did upon arrival was walk out of the relationship that the natal soul had been in for more than two decades.

If you attempted suicide, you may have miraculously survived and even feel angry and/or delighted that the body is still here. Anger may be leftover from the natal soul. Delight may be the walk-in soul expressing gratitude that the body survived the ordeal and that the transfer was successful. Many people whose soul walked in during a near-death (or "flat line" experience in which the body was actually pronounced dead) say that they do not want to be on

Earth or feel like they do not belong here. To me, this is an indication that either the natal soul's energy has not cleared the brain or the body's cellular memory, or that the natal soul did not cross over and is still hanging out in the electromagnetic field of the body it left.

A walk-in soul comes from a realm of instant manifestation, which does not have the chaos, limiting belief systems, and "domestication" (as Don Miguel Ruiz calls it in *The Four Agreements*) of Earth life. A newly-arrived starseed soul can become distracted by all this stuff and not be able to move forward with its mission for many years—unfortunately some never do move into expressing their divine mission. Realizing that you have walked in can be the missing piece of the puzzle that helps you untangle the knots that have held you back. Even though I have been reluctant to share my story (for fear that my family and friends would think I am totally off my rocker), I feel that I must help walk-ins unravel the mystery and learn why they are here. If people are aware of what has or is happening to them, the adjustment process will be much less painful and the work of the walk-in soul can begin much more quickly.

If you got sidetracked by embracing the faulty thinking of human consciousness and automated behaviors that are part of the social conditioning the prior soul experienced, you can still heal and move forward. All suffering is a result of a brain that needs healing. The soul is perfect and cannot be anything other than one with God—it is part of Divine Source. We may have camouflaged our divinity, denied its existence, or layered junk on top of it, but the essence of perfection is who we truly are. I like what Kenji Kumara said when I had him as a guest on We Are One in Spirit Podcast in October 2012. "Suffering is not needed. When we remember our perfect and whole state of being and operate in that mindset, we raise our vibration and begin to influence others in a positive way. They may be healed just by being in our presence. We may lay hands on them and they are cleared of limiting beliefs and begin to resonate with their divine truth and raise their own vibration." Access the show with Kenji at http://goo.gl/6B857.

After learning this, I began to walk in the truth that I am perfect and one with God. Each day the goal of my meditation is to reach a place of feeling bliss, joy, love, and gratitude—even if it is only for a few minutes. This practice has a tremendous effect on healing the brain that has picked up the habit of believing lies about who we are. The brain governs the thought processes, emotions, and functions of the body. If the brain is filled with light, the whole body is filled with light. We will look at this type of healing in Chapter 7.

Chapter 2 ~ What is a Walk-in?

A walk-in is a soul that has walked into an adult body rather than the body of an infant. The natal soul—the one that entered the body at the infant stage—normally walks out at the same time that a new soul walks in. Unlike the possession that occurs when an Earthbound entity forces its way in uninvited, this exchange of souls is done with permission, and there are no hostile takeovers.

I smile whenever I talk to someone who craves to have a walk-in or soul exchange. If only they knew how hard it was for some of us to go through such a thing!

Fortunately, today's swapping and merging of soul essences is not the "trial-and-error" cosmic experiment that it seemed to be for many of us "forerunners" in the 1980s and '90s, when an increase in soul exchanges started being noticed. There is now a collaborative effort and better communication between those of us in body and those galactic beings who are helping to facilitate the integration process, which is joining our multidimensional selves into a cohesive expression of oneness. Soul exchanges today are more gradual, occurring over the span of many years rather than the "in one day and out the next" scenario some people had a few decades ago.

If you are desirous of the spiritual bliss that accompanies a successful walk-in integration, you will be happy to know that it is not just a select few who are experiencing soul upgrades. Humans are being transformed by receiving into their physical body the energy of some multidimensional aspect of consciousness or a future (vibrating at a higher octave) version of themselves. The pieces of ourselves that fragmented as a result of the trauma of our belief in separation are also being reassembled as we move away from separation (polarity) and move toward oneness with All That Is. This is what some call the "ascension." Our galactic alignment exposes us and the Earth to the influences of other planets. These cosmic rays introduce multidimensional energy that begins to shift the body to hold universal frequencies of higher octaves. This is having a genetic effect upon humans. It is restoring the blueprint of the 12-strand DNA model that was modified eons ago. This modification cut us off from our multi-dimensional awareness and created duality (right/wrong, good/bad, male/female), causing us to live in the illusion of separation.

We are constantly receiving information through our skin— the largest organ of our body—but we are conditioned to believe that if we cannot see, hear, taste, smell, or touch something, then it does not exist. Yet, we know that discerning abilities exist even beyond our intuition. We are constantly receiving information through the sensory receptors of our skin, which in our divine form was originally part of our autonomic system. These sensors went offline because we stopped using them. Animals know when a tsunami is coming, and they get to the highest hill while humans, who ignore their higher guidance, stay in the danger zone until it is too late and they get washed away.

Humans have never been comfortable with things they cannot explain. Many are not able to accept supernatural occurrences and ideas because their filters of what is possible prevent them from believing in something outside of the socially-accepted norm. They fear rejection from those who lack understanding regarding the multifaceted soul; they do not know that we are spirit having a human experience. That is why many people do not talk about such things as near-death experiences, seeing ghosts, or being taken aboard a spacecraft. Fortunately, people have begun to open up and report what has personally happened to them; and thanks to mainstream media (although distorted), the belief in an afterlife, communication with the deceased, and interaction with our galactic family is gaining acceptance in American culture.

Prior to the 1970s, no one had heard of a near-death experience (NDE) and the term was not even in our vernacular. We were just getting accustomed to that phenomenon when we started hearing about walk-ins or soul exchanges. And, here I am embracing the very real experience of working with our galactic family to help raise the vibration of Earth and the consciousness of humanity. Some readers may find these concepts a bit far-fetched. But, bear with me and let's see if I can shed enough logic on the topic to help you open to something bigger than the view you currently have of yourself and the life you are now experiencing.

An idea gains validity when enough people talk about it in a way that makes it "safe" to accept. The knowledge that some souls walk into an adult body rather than being born into an infant body is a new concept to many people. It is probably not something you have discussed at the dinner table with your in-laws. However, people have been reporting these occurrences for many decades, especially since the harmonic convergence on August 16 and 17, 1987—the world's first globally synchronized meditation, announced by José Argüelles.

Once people know what a walk-in experience is and enough walk-ins overcome the confusion that sometimes takes place when a soul exchange occurs, society will see this as a common experience. Why is this important? Because soon after a walk-in occurs, the person involved usually begins to experience or create huge lifestyle modifications.

Maxine Taylor began her astrological studies in 1966. In 1968, she became Georgia's first licensed astrologer. In 1970, she got astrology legalized in Atlanta, and spearheaded the establishment of the Atlanta Board of Astrology Examiners. In her book, *Earthbound,* Maxine Taylor states: "The combination of the cell memory of the walk-out and the advanced psychic ability and knowledge of the walk-in can be confusing and frustrating. But, ultimately, these energies balance and you will be able to express your mission." Maxine's passion is working with walk-ins and helping them understand their walk-out and walk-in lives by understanding their natal and walk-in charts.

At first, walk-ins may feel differently about their family members and friends. They may change jobs, redecorate their homes, or relocate. Even the style of clothes they wear may change drastically. In some cases, these shifts in feelings are gradual and relatively subtle. But for others, the shifts may be immediate and dramatic. If the person is not aware that a soul exchange is occurring, the experience can be very disorienting. Having people understand and accept the phenomena is part of the integration process that restores wholeness to the individual. Thus, books like this one are intended to bring knowledge of soul exchanges into the mainstream consciousness and help walk-in souls move forward and begin to offer the healing gifts they have brought with them.

In her 1979 best-selling book, *Strangers Among Us*, Ruth Montgomery indicated that walk-ins are beings who have attained adequate awareness of the deceptions posed by Earth life. This ability to see through the illusion allows them to forego the process of birth and childhood, incarnating directly into adult bodies. Though Ruth did not consider herself to be a walk-in, she was the first person in modern times to write about the subject. In her later book, *Threshold to Tomorrow*, she named sixteen walk-ins, and described their walk-in experiences. Among these was my dear friend, Carol Parrish-Harra. In her autobiographical book, *Messengers of Hope*, Carol wrote that walk-ins are spiritual messengers who enter behind the veil of another personality at certain opportune moments for service to humanity. She, herself, walked in over thirty years ago.

When a new soul comes into physical embodiment through the walk-in process, the original soul normally (but not always) leaves, moving on to other experiences in non-physical worlds, just as it would if it had gone through a physical death. The incoming soul either walks along with the natal soul or assumes full responsibility for the human body, and for completing the life in progress.

Some people might believe that a body is overtaken by a demon or disincarnate spirit in this process. There are no hostile takeovers! A walk-in can only take place with the full agreement of both the outgoing and incoming souls. A walk-in is the exact opposite of a low-vibrating possession because of the positive associations it has with the Light. In fact, the walk-in soul is typically more evolved than the natal soul. Carrying out a pre-arranged contract with a harmonized counterpart, soul exchanges are done with mutual consent to move both the walk-in and walk-out souls forward in spiritual evolution and bring a higher vibration to the earth, helping the planet ascend into purer planes of consciousness.

Many soul exchanges occur during exit points such as near-death experiences, surgeries, out-of-body experiences, dissociative episodes, dark nights of the soul, periods of unconsciousness, or other traumatic events. In the past, however, most walk-ins were not consciously aware of what was happening. That is because the incoming soul inherits the natal soul's memory stored in the cells of the physical body, and souls on Earth are behind a veil of forgetfulness and illusion. Thankfully, that veil is thinning more and more.

Today, more and more walk-ins are coming in consciously aware of what is happening, and they may have conscious awareness that a soul exchange is about to or has taken place. They may even remember many of the details of the transitional process from both perspectives—that of the Earth plane and the higher dimension. In such cases, the exchange is made in a cooperative manner, and there is less upset as they acclimate, integrate, heal the body, overcome addictions, and resolve remaining past soul issues. Those souls usually have a good idea of the spiritual assignment they have come to complete and are ready to get on with life.

So what is a walk-in anyway? There is both a simple and a complex answer. Simple, if you understand the multi-dimensional aspect of a soul (persona or expression of the Divine) existing simultaneously on parallel planes; simple, if you consider that Divine Source is everywhere and that we are individuations of that creative essence. Some refer to this omnipotent, omniscient, omnipresent energy as "God," so I'll use that term a few times in this book. The answer is simple if you can accept that being born into a body is not the *only* way a soul can enter the Earth, and that death is not the *only* way a soul can leave this world. Similar to how we might rearrange our furniture, change clothes, trade cars, or move to a new house, the essence of a soul from one dimension is able to come and go from the third dimension known as Earth.

However, the answer is complicated when trying to explain all the ways that soul exchanges, co-habitations, soul braids/merges, soul over-lighting/draping, soul upgrades, and cosmic downloads can happen. (We will look at these in Chapter 2.) Just as creation is limitless and ever expanding, so is our eternal expression of Divine Source and the experiences we can have. There is no way I can cover this topic completely, but I do hope to give an overview of each of these and help you know that you are supported in accomplishing your mission.

All who live in this reality follow paths set by our predecessors. Walk-ins arrive at each evolutionary step in advance of the masses, adding clarity and stability while leaving a clearly marked pathway as they move forward in service to humanity. These "way-showers" embark upon rugged terrain, determine what needs to be done to safely navigate and create the necessary changes, and then assist others in integrating the vibrational shift. As they refine their own personal journey, they become the model for others to follow.

Walk-ins are these pathfinders! We are personally aware of the subtle nudges we are receiving, knowing we are well prepared for each moment as it unfolds. Much like dolphins that receive and send signals to one another, we transmit our unique signal that activates the information encoded in our cells. Many walk-ins carry symbols and encodings within their personal field. These codes automatically help others gracefully integrate higher vibrational energy into a physical body. When we connect with another, we share our puzzle piece, expand our experience, and we are all changed.

Common Types of Walk-In Experiences

There are several different types of walk-ins. Some exchanges are between two unrelated souls (differing soul groups, monads, or oversouls) who have partnered for a particular (or multiple) incarnation. Other walk-ins involve primary soul mates from a group of souls (matrix) governed by the same monad, the perfect God essence or consciousness. Much like the brain is to the body, a monad is the highly-developed nucleus of a system. The monad is the ultimate guidance or control center of a group of souls that includes twin flames, soul mates, and soul aspects such as personalities and archetypes: inner child, the critical parent, the wounded healer, etc. A monad supplies the life-force, love, and attention needed to maintain an embodied soul's existence on Earth as well as in non-physical realms. Your personal monad is responsible for your evolution as it ensures that all aspects of your being work in harmony toward soul integration. In spiritual terms, one monad contains twelve oversouls and each oversoul has twelve personalities (144 soul aspects).

Some bodies hold space on the Earth plane for many souls in a group to pass through over a lifetime. These "revolving door" walk-ins are like an inn where a soul or soul aspect may stay for a short while and then move on when the mission is complete. You will meet some of them in this book.

There are many variations of walk-ins and soul exchanges, so do not get caught up in labeling your experience. Each one is unique, depending upon the life situation of the natal soul, the background of the incoming spirit, and Earth's evolutionary condition at the time of the walk-in. If you are a walk-in, use this book as a reference to understand your own experience.

Soul Exchanges

Before incarnation, an agreement is made between two souls to share a body during separate periods of time in order for each soul to accomplish more in one Earth lifetime. Soul exchanges take place when one soul walks out of a physical body at the same time the companion soul walks in.

When the first soul's mission is complete and it no longer needs the body, it may choose to transfer the "real estate" (physical body) over to its companion soul rather than allowing the body to die. Therefore, the walk-in experience is a very wise use of "human resources." Most families will not even know the natal soul has left. However, they may note many changes in the person's life. My close family suspected I was having an emotional breakdown of sorts. But, since my walk-in occurred at age forty, I was able to pass it off as a mid-life crisis, which is the best understanding I had about what was happening at the time.

The natal soul that takes the body through the formative infant and childhood years may have a difficult life because that soul has asked for a "crash course" in order to speed up the evolutionary process. This life of hardships may create a very strong urge to leave the body when things get really painful. This is the signal for the walk-in/out process to begin. As the natal soul prepares to walk out, it may arrange for its exit by creating health problems, addictions, emotional issues, illness, or an accident. Some souls who are extremely desperate to leave may even attempt suicide. After all, humans do not typically want to leave a life that is happy and going well.

The Death Wish

Rebirthers such as Leonard Orr and Sondra Ray refer to a subconscious death wish that every human has. It is part of the collective human psyche. We notice this polarity when we wish to live fully. Both are valid self-expressions to be embraced, not judged.

The death wish includes beliefs such as these:

- I love God and want to be with Him. I need to die to be with God
- It is too hard here, and I want to go "home"
- There is value in suffering; all humans suffer

It is important to know that you did not do anything "wrong" by having a death urge. Becoming aware of it is a positive step of growth in your self-realization. The key is to simply accept that there was, up until this particular moment of choice, a part of you wishing to die. Affirm, accept, and love that part of yourself. Then, choose to live fully.

A soul makes commitments to other people, organizations, institutions, and philosophies and then goes about the rest of its Earth life trying to keep them. When a walk-in takes the body, all the commitments, vows, and promises made by the walk-out soul are still operating underneath the surface. It reminds me of the time I saw my twelve-year-old grandson give his toddler-age brother a video remote control that was not connected to the system. The younger one *thought* he was playing and controlling the action. If you have ever tried playing a game on Xbox, PlayStation, Wii, or some other system while there's a toddler begging to play too, you can appreciate this analogy.

Without clearing the commitments of the natal soul, the walk-in soul lives in "demo" mode. He thinks he is controlling the action he sees on the screen of his life, but he is actually going through the motions without realizing that another program is running the show. The walk-in may rebel against these programs that stem from the natal soul's family, co-workers, bosses, spouses, children, pets, and friends. This "information" may register as an illness or discomfort in the physical body.

The ego mind always wants to know *why*. The answer is often multifaceted, even multidimensional and is outside the comprehension and knowledge of the linear, ego mind. You may or may not know consciously what is holding you back. However, it can be very helpful to discover and expose these "bad messages" in order to speak the command to be released from a commitment your soul did not make. Maxine Taylor's book, *Move into the Magic*, offers excellent resources for doing just that. Maxine is an ordained trans-denominational minister, a Reconnective Healing Practitioner, and a Matrix Energetics healer. (See http://www.maxinetaylor.com.)

When a subconscious "death wish" continues after the walk-out soul has left the body, it can cause the walk-in's mission to get stuck or even be aborted if the life of the body ends because the core issue was not dealt with. That is why it is so important for walk-ins to have support to keep the body safe during the adjustment phase.

Thankfully, not all walk-outs create drama when they are ready to leave. If a soul has learned what it needed to learn and accomplished its purpose, it can choose to "pass the baton" to an incoming soul without impairing the body through an unconscious death urge.

Hannah Beaconsfield, the author of *Welcome to Planet Earth*, refers to the walk-in phenomenon as "spirit replacement" and likens it to a long-running Broadway show in which the leading actors play out their contracts and are then replaced by other actors. The new actors bring their particular qualities to the parts and there are some changes, but the "show goes on."

While the walk-out soul is taking its final bow, the walk-in soul is arranging for its debut. More than likely this partner soul has been serving as guide for the natal soul, or is at least familiar with all that has occurred thus far in the physical incarnation.

The walk-in maintains the lower three chakras and functions of the body and picks up where the natal soul left off. It overlays the imprint for its own spiritual mission as it connects to the upper four chakras. Even though there is compatibility between the two souls, there is often an adjustment period in which the body must acclimate to the higher vibrations of the incoming soul that hails from a realm where there is no linear time.

So, what happens to the natal soul when it walks out? Some run to the light in a mad dash for relief. Thus, they are not involved in the work that is being initiated by the walk-in soul. In other cases, the natal soul remains close by to guide the walk-in through social interactions and life situations it left pending. However, the natal soul has been conditioned with the distortions, illusions, and dysfunctions of the 3-D world and is probably not the best guide for the walk-in soul to rely upon. Other times, the natal soul may stay in the auric field to observe and learn lessons while the new soul picks up the pieces and begins to heal and resolve issues and beliefs that created the exit point for the natal soul. Partner souls only want the best for one another. A positive auric attachment can be a benefit to the newly-arrived soul if the walk-out is emotionally detached from the outcome and is able to offer unbiased guidance from a higher perspective. However, the natal soul can also cloud the judgment of the walk-in soul by influencing decisions or trying to maintain control over the life it has left.

Soul Braids or Walk-Alongs

Souls are individuations of the Divine Cosmic Intelligence and are therefore multidimensional. It may be hard for some to fathom that humans have counterparts that exist in other planes and realms of consciousness where there is peaceful cooperation among all beings of light. In this century, we are seeing a lot of changes on Earth, as well as in our experience as humans. One of those changes is the incoming of multidimensional aspects of our souls. These are called "soul braids" or "walk-alongs" in which the energy of an additional soul joins the Earth mission but the original personality/soul does not leave. Instead, the two souls integrate. There may be name changes as a result. There are certainly physical, emotional, and cognitive changes. Sometimes companion souls move in and out of the body as needed. One will hold the body while the other takes care of matters in another dimension or level of vibrational consciousness, and then swap places or peacefully cohabitate and collaborate on a project for which both souls are needed.

There are times when an aspect of a soul will come to aid the embodied portion of the soul by offering special skills. I experienced this when writing *Shifting into Purer Consciousness ~ Integrating Spiritual Transformation with the Human Experience*. I was draped by a higher aspect of my soul from the eighth or ninth dimension. I felt this energy around me for twelve consecutive days and enjoyed a time of bliss like no other I had experienced prior. Even after the "high" left, I recognized an empowerment throughout the writing, editing, and publishing process. That aspect of my soul was integrated by the time the book was published.

During times of soul braiding, a person can become very intense and focused on accomplishing their divine purpose. To help facilitate this mission, they may exhibit healing abilities, keen psychic sensitivity (empathy), strong and accurate intuition, and other spiritual gifts.

Soul braids can be formed in any number of combinations. Sometimes a soul braid is an oversoul merge in which a higher aspect of the same soul will download into the body and become part of a life experience, either temporarily or lifelong. Before I knew what a soul braid was, I referred to this experience as a changing of my spirit guides. I seem to feel, sense, and hear my guidance differently when this occurs.

An oversoul is a future self or higher frequency (think of musical or vibrational octaves) that is purer in consciousness and free of the polarity that characterizes three-dimensional life on Earth. When someone is said to be living in the third dimension, it means they are operating from the lower three chakras and have no concept of their multi-dimensional aspects.

There are cases when two or more souls may share a body, or its electromagnetic field, for a season or a lifetime. Entities, which are both detrimental and beneficial soul aspects, can attach themselves to the body or aura of an incarnated soul.

When a person is abused, a soul can fragment to allow other aspects of their personality to come in and help deal with the stress. Thus, it makes sense that dissociative experiences are part of a spiritual journey rather than a mental or emotional disorder.

When two or more enlightened or evolved souls share a body or auric space, there is the kind of cooperation, peace, and harmony that we humans experience when working on a project as a team of qualified professionals. By the same token, there are cases in which we see lower aspects of a soul attached to and influencing an embodied soul. We want to avoid this and free ourselves of the potential for this to occur. When we forgive others, we heal wounds and close the portals that allow such contamination. I believe this is why Jesus's primary teachings were about forgiveness and love. These entity attachments are the kind he "cast out" of the people to whom he ministered. Like the Christ, we raise our vibration by focusing on joy and bliss and by recognizing our oneness with God and All That Is—even these lower aspects of our souls. When we "cast them out" we are actually integrating them or putting them into their proper perspective by not allowing them to rule and reign over our thoughts, emotions, and actions. Then, the higher avatar self takes the wheel and calls the shots.

In the new world level of consciousness, the personality (ego or duality) and all the holographic aspects of the soul are reunited, and all chakras are blended into one unified field or column of light. This is known as the zero-point field or the trinity form.

Temporary Blending or Place Holding

The body is a vehicle, temple, or dwelling place for a soul. You may loan your car, rent out your house, or have someone live in your home while you are away. You may hire someone to come in and clean your house while you rest. You may have had some remodeling done to your dwelling while you were still living in it. My husband and I did this when we gutted our kitchen in 2007. We were without a sink for two weeks of the seven-week project. Washing dishes in the bathtub was a trip with no luggage; however, the finished project was amazing and I still enjoy the results. Compare this remodeling example to what a short- or long-term soul braid might accomplish. A soul braid may result in a miraculous healing of the body from a terminal illness, or it may create a life shift that the embodied soul was not able to achieve.

Another reason for a temporary blending occurs when one soul wants to experience something on Earth and then agrees to walk out when that venture is complete. Later on, another soul may come and experience what it needs. A soul braid may also be another version of your own soul coming in to assist the planet with evolution.

Because the body's main function is to serve as a vehicle for expressing the various individuations of Source energy, multiple walk-ins or soul braids may occur in one body during a lifetime. Remember: these events are always agreements made between soul aspects, even if those involved are not consciously aware of the negotiation.

There may be times when a more evolved soul or higher aspect of someone's soul holds the body as a marker soul while the natal soul does astral travel and accomplishes a task in another realm. This is a temporary assignment. When the natal soul returns, the swap is again made, but the individual may not notice it as much because the body has become accustomed to the higher vibration of the marker soul, and is able to accommodate the natal soul's frequency, which is higher than it was when it first left. Why is it higher? The soul is perfect and now that the second soul has cleared the body of many negative imprints, the natal soul can vibrate with less obstruction.

Many people are experiencing some profound shifts as we are ascending in consciousness. Next, let's look at some experiences that could mimic a soul exchange, but are something different.

Chapter 3 ~ What Is NOT a Walk-in?

There are many life-changing events that can mimic a walk-in or soul exchange. After describing what a walk-in *is*, I feel it is important to define what a walk-in or soul exchange is *not*.

A walk-in or soul exchange is not the same as a near-death or other spiritually-transforming experience, soul activation, mid-life crisis, Kundalini awakening, or dark night of the soul. It is not an ET or angelic visitation, or the baptism in the Holy Spirit. It is not the same as channeling a spirit being, having a dissociative episode, or getting a download of higher vibrational energy. However, a soul exchange can certainly occur during any one of these experiences.

Activations and Downloads

Our soul is perfect, regardless of what we experience here on Earth. However, in order to help us realize our divinity, we may encounter a "bump up" in energy that helps us attain a new spiritual level of awareness, which is really exposing the beauty of what is already there.

From time to time, you may receive a download of spiritual information or higher truth. These downloads are similar to how our computer automatically updates its software or operating system. This occurs as the body is able to receive, anchor, and function with the faster vibration of the monad, oversoul, and advanced versions of your soul.

These downloads seem to come randomly. Like the arcade game where you toss a token onto the shelf with other tokens that have begun to stack up, you hope that the tokens you add to the pile will cause an avalanche of tokens to fall into the bin below where you can collect your windfall. This "build up" of energy may go unnoticed until the shelf starts to get full. That is when we begin to encounter difficult situations or feel a heaviness that indicates it is time to break through to the next level and begin to embody a higher octave frequency or future self.

Once the upgrades start, they will continue, and you may get mini activations at any time, with or without warning. You may get a "hit" in your senses that something is about to happen. You may hear a buzzing sound in your ears, feel light-headed or dizzy, sense an expansion of energy around your head or heart, have hypersensitivity in your skin, or just know intuitively that you are about to get a motherload! When you notice any of these symptoms, tune in and ask your guidance what is occurring and how you can assist. The trick here is to be aware of what is happening so you can cooperate and make the process easier and faster.

Many people are afraid of what some call the "shadow side" because they start experiencing new feelings or desires— erotic or sexual energy arising—that are considered inappropriate by social conditioning. This is a natural occurrence when your heart is open to others and your chakras are allowing energy to flow freely. Supernatural gifts also start coming forth because this is how we were originally programmed to operate had we not been brainwashed to believe that we are limited and puny subjects of a punishing God.

Higher octave energy is anchored within the personality and body as a result of the unveiling of the authentic self; therefore, a period of integration may be required as higher vibrational frequencies are integrated into the physical body. These frequencies are actually restructuring the DNA to support the light body that we are all in the process of building. One of the most notable symptoms of integration is the need for more rest or sleep. Thankfully, these events do not typically cause the huge shift in personality that a soul exchange often does. They do bring an expansion of consciousness—a new or heightened awareness that we are spirit beings having a human experience, and the incoming fire tends to quickly advance the recipient forward on his or her spiritual path.

Many times, the higher current will upset the ego or dislodge lower-vibrating entities. These immature aspects of the personality need to be lovingly "re-parented" or trained not to interfere with the ascension process. The end result is that we are being transformed by the renewing of our mind or healing of our brains and emotions. Thus, we gain a greater ability to recognize that we are one in and with spirit.

Activation of Light Languages

Part of the work that walk-ins are here to do is to restore communication between humans and galactic beings. We do this as we begin to connect with our divine source within our Sacred Heart, maintain and keep our personal energy field clear of emotional or mental debris that disrupts the cellular communication of the body.

There is a level of supernatural speaking known as a light language, spirit language, or star language that carries frequencies of light that contain cosmic or galactic information. A lot of walk-ins (and people who are not even familiar with the walk-in concept) are spontaneously receiving this language. It may sound like gibberish with a sing-song lilt, much like Mandarin or oriental Asian, but I've been told that some languages are pre-Atlantian and pre-Lemurian galactic dialects.

The Native Americans have known about star languages for longer than there has been a Pentecostal denomination. There are similarities between the experience of being baptized in the Holy Spirit, evidenced by the speaking in tongues, and the activation of these light languages.

If you were raised in church, you may have come across scripture that talks about the day of the Pentecost in which tongues of fire fell upon a culturally diverse gathering of people, who then began speaking languages that they had not learned. This incident allowed a linguistically diverse group of people to rise above their language barrier and communicate without translators. (Later in this book, you will read about a modern-day walk-in's experience in supernaturally receiving the ability to speak the Russian language.)

In the early 1990s, I became interested in the gifts of the Spirit mentioned in the Bible. I prayed every day to be filled with the Holy Spirit and to receive all nine gifts mentioned in chapter 12 of I Corinthians. Soon, I started sensing and even sometimes seeing spirits. I had faith to believe in things that others thought impossible, and witnessed the manifestation of miracles. Gifts of healing soon appeared when I laid hands on people; I began to prophesize, have dreams and visions, and "know" things about people that had not been revealed to me.

In 1993, my prayer partner came to my house. She mentioned that she had received the gift of speaking in tongues that allows one to speak from the heart without the logical mind knowing what is being spoken. Since I was so hungry to experience more of the Holy Spirit, she thought it would be easy for me to receive what she called a "prayer language." In simple faith, I let the energy pour forth that I had been bubbling up inside me. The words I spoke sounded like a real language and not just incoherent babbling. I trusted that it was indeed the gift of tongues, and continued to use it in my prayer times throughout the 1990s. Soon, I had a sense of what I was praying for when I used this language. People seem to be receiving these gifts today without all the wrestling and time my natal soul spent seeking this experience!

I worked so hard to bring forth these gifts, and then gave them all up after my walk-in when everything in my life shifted dramatically. After I left organized religion in the early 2000s and stopped having a daily prayer time, I practically forgot about these gifts. You snooze, you lose; or so I thought. When I was in Sedona in 2012, I met a Native American grandmother named Sakina Blue Star, who invited me to participate in her medicine wheel ceremony. She opened the circle by calling on the four directions. As soon as I heard her speak a greeting in her star language, my solar plexus and throat started contracting and I began groaning as I held back and tried not to interrupt Sakina. However, she immediately recognized what was occurring and asked me to share the message that Spirit was bringing through. I burst into my light language, gave a message none of us understood, and then started sobbing. Sakina recognized my language as an ancient tribal dialect she had heard one other person speak.

Certain light languages carry frequencies that contain cosmic or galactic messages or codes. I sensed that my message had something to do with the Native Americans who suffered and died along the Trail of Tears in the mid- to late-1830s. I recognized that there were spirits who were ready to cross over. So much for the gift of discerning spirits; I did not know that I had picked up the earthbound spirits of about 250 of these ancestors.

Once I got home, I felt sad and depressed. Plus, I was having terrible mood swings, and knew that I was carrying more than my personal energy. I kept thinking that maybe some lower-vibrating issues were coming up to be cleared as I integrated higher vibrations from the downloads of energy I received while in Sedona. After about two weeks of emotional agony, I was lying face down on our back deck begging my guides for clarity and help. That is when I began to have a vision and an internal telepathic dialog with a Native American elder. Immediately, within my own mind, I found myself facilitating a ceremony that released these precious Native American souls into the light. It was like watching a movie as I observed what was happening. It had been almost twelve years since I had seen dreams and visions like this. In fact, all the gifts I had been endowed with in the 1990s seemed to be reactivating of their own accord.

Since that day, I have used my light language in rituals, prayer sessions, and meditation on a regular basis. I wish I were not so thick-headed and could learn my lessons without such drama. This, too, shall pass as I become a clearer channel!

Impartation or Energy Transfers

A fully-integrated walk-in can gracefully carry accelerated cosmic frequencies, maintain his or her personal space (about 18-24 inches surrounding the body), and hold open a field of energy for others to access. People can sometimes feel this energy emanating from a high-vibe soul.

The Bible talks about the impartation of gifts. This is referring to a transfer of energy from one person, who is carrying a high frequency, to another person who is willing to align or resonate or "match pitch" with a higher frequency. Physical and emotional healing can occur through the transfer of energy that comes from laying hands on a person or raising frequencies to create a "pool of energy" that someone can step into—even remotely. Kenji Kumara talked about this kind of transfer of energy in the podcast he and I did. (Download the brain wave activation audio here: http://goo.gl/6B857.) I facilitated a workshop hosted by the Nashville Psychic Meetup Group in January 2013. We built a pool of energy and held the field open for nearly four hours during which the energy was so intense that everyone there could sense it in a tangible way.

After several months of coaching via telephone, a client and I met at a coffee shop in person for the first time. When I arrived at the meeting that day, I was not on my game because of the traffic and frustrating parking issues I encountered on my way. However, after a few minutes of chatting with the client I attuned with his frequency and got back to the higher vibration that is normal for me.

We had been talking about what had happened to him a couple of years prior. He wondered why his body had vibrated and felt like it was unwinding as it shook involuntarily during meditation. He also had started speaking a strange language and smelled beautiful fragrances. At times, his forehead felt like it was being stretched open or expanded. The reason for these strange sensations? The body and its nervous system were being rewired to handle an influx of high-frequency energy from higher dimensions.

During our in-person coaching session, I sensed that he was about to receive an energy download, but I did not mention this to him. As we parted ways, we shared a quick hug. When two people physically touch one another, their energy fields meet and merge. This can last for just a moment or for days (or a lifetime) depending upon how open both parties are to continuing to allow one another's energy to remain in a shared field. Within minutes of that innocent hug, the energy download that I sensed was forthcoming started manifesting for him. He texted to say that he felt so dizzy he could not drive his car.

Neither of us had expected this. Our guides do not always understand the linear time that governs Earth life and they can initiate an energy download—even at a time when it is not convenient for us to process it. I encouraged him to talk with his guides and let them know this process would need to wait until he got home and went into meditation. The symptoms lessened within half an hour, but he continued to integrate the energy for more than a month afterward. The next thing I knew, I was experiencing a strong Kundalini rising that lasted for over two months, and revolutionized my life. My relationships improved, the cells of my body cast off detrimental energy imprints, and I began to experience a greater amount of bliss than ever in my life.

As a side note, there are times when I "hold space" for a client who is going through a transition. When I hold space for someone, I create a joint field with him or her and allow access to my personal field so they can connect with a high-frequency. I only do this with clients and friends, who truly want to change and simply need a power boost to help them connect with the quantum field. Otherwise, it can be draining for me. I certainly do not recommend that you open your field like this until you understand how to manage your personal field of energy. Be sure you do not allow people to deposit in your aura whatever negativity they are clearing.

This type of impartation or energy transfer happens between me and my husband all the time. If one of us gets in a bad mood, the other immediately feels it. There are times when we either have to help one another get our vibration back up, or go to separate areas of our home or leave the premises to avoid energy contamination. That is a situation that two empaths commonly encounter when living together. If we are both vibrating in alignment with the I AM Presence, we get so high we become giddy. Thankfully, we are able to recognize what is playing out and can quickly resolve whatever is causing the foul mood—usually one of us has picked up the energy of someone we were exposed to when we let our energetic guard down in public. Or, one of us is living in the emotional energy of the past rather than in the now moment—easy to do when clearing unwanted patterns from the psyche.

As far as what you might expect after you experience a download from your soul matrix, I cannot say. It varies from one person to the next. For me, once my vibration is raised through a download/transfer, I feel invigorated, light, and carefree, and I notice a positive shift in my overall perspective. Whatever discord I encountered, prior to the download, is dissolved. I get a euphoric feeling of love in my heart center and can feel my body, chakras, and aura vibrating or pulsating with waves of energy. My sensory perception is keener and I feel more loving toward everyone. I call it the "new puppy" syndrome because it makes me want to hug and squeeze total strangers!

Be aware that downloads may be preceded by depression, anger, or emotional/mental discord. That is because when the upgrade/download is starting to penetrate the aura, it pushes up emotional energy that has served its purpose and is ready to be released. Higher-frequency energy pushes out fear and births new realities. It is a good idea to visualize or intend the ultraviolet flame of transmutation around you whenever you are experiencing discord. The job of this flame is to remove anything that is in the way of expressing your authentic soul essence. You do not have to process the old stuff that comes up. Acknowledge it—even thank it for the role it served—but do not let it distract you from living in the now moment. Try to stay in your new blissful high vibe.

You are the only person who can open or close your heart and mind, and you can do that as fast or slowly as you choose, regardless of whether you are receiving a spiritual download. The invitation is always open for you to express your true self and live in bliss and joy. Proceed with love in all you do. Love will gracefully change whatever needs to shift.

Rising Kundalini

A profound Kundalini episode, which sometimes produces an explosive change in someone's life, may be mistaken for a soul exchange. Kundalini energy is hot and expansive and can be triggered unexpectedly. Do not be surprised if it ignites sensual feelings or sexual desires; Kundalini is primordial energy from which all things are created.

We live in a culture that has a love-hate/come-here-go- away relationship to sex. It is used in advertising campaigns, movies, songs, and jokes, which seems to indicate that sex is to be highly sought after. On the opposite end of the spectrum, families, society, and religions frown upon those who have or enjoy sex—especially if it is done outside the accepted social norm of male/female monogamous relationships. Most people never make the connection that their sexual energy is life force energy and therefore the key to their creativity and vitality. In honoring your true self, you must honor this energy that is always alive within you.

I invite my coaching clients to simply feel what they feel and not be ashamed or afraid of these "shadow side" feelings. Just because you feel sexual energy does not mean you have to have sex. You can use sexual or erotic energy to create anything you want and enhance every aspect of your life.

Erotic energy can be moved about within the body, and you can generate more of it. Because you can harness this energy, direct it, and cause it to take form, it is definitely useful when participating in an artistic expression or attempting to manifest something. It can move you to another state of awareness from which you can create anything from a beautiful piece of music to a new job. That is the whole point of having sexual energy. Without it, there is no birth or creation of anything.

In Chapter 11 of *Think and Grow Rich*, Napolean Hill writes about the mystery of sex transmutation.

When driven by this [sex] desire, men develop keenness of imagination, courage, will-power, persistence, and creative ability unknown to them at other times ... When harnessed, and redirected ... , [it] may be used as powerful creative forces in literature, art, or in any other profession ... it should be given an outlet through forms of expression which enrich the body, mind, and spirit of man.

During meditation (or at any time—even unprovoked) you may feel sexual energy moving through your entire body in waves, filling and activating the lower energy centers with desire. And since creativity is within you all the time and is part of who you are, you can channel it for purposes other than having sex. There is a big difference between having an "erotic life" and having a "sex life." Having sex or an orgasm is not even half of what it means to be energized by erotic energy. Releasing the energy through sexual activity can actually *lessen* it. When you do not disburse sexual energy through orgasm, it builds and naturally channels into creative expression and helps you do things you might not have had the energy or boldness to do before. The key is to channel the energy rather than allowing it to dictate your actions or make you a slave to your sex drive. I am not suggesting that you repress or resist sexual urges—that action is fear-based or guilt-driven, which serves no useful purpose other than causing frustration that slows down spiritual progress. Instead, harness this energy and infuse it into everything you do. Your work and life mission can be inspired and your family and friendships can be influenced positively as you interact from a heart filled with love that is activated by sexual energy. From grocery shopping to writing a blog post, it can bring bliss, creativity, and joy as it invites you to enjoy the present moment.

Being under the influence of sexual energy is like being drunk or drugged; it can inspire you to take risks and do things you would not do otherwise. It can lessen the fear you might feel about taking the next step in a business venture or some other opportunity. Before you can direct strong sexual energy toward other useful pursuits, you must be able to hold and flow the energy in your personal space and body. This can be done as you connect with your sacred heart center in the *now* moment, without being distracted by the constant chatter of the mind.

When you feel sexual energy stirring within you, stay in a space of awareness and feel it as it courses through your body. Notice the way it pulsates and provides a sense of power within you. Simply contain it and allow it to revitalize and heal the body, lift depression, open blockages, dissolve sexual hang-ups, and spark new ideas. As you hold this powerful presence, you can begin to direct the energy toward some creative endeavor by using thought or intention.

Ultimately the energy is within you, and can be activated without the influence of another person. However, tantric exploration, practicing heart connection, or sending/receiving energy with another person can increase this flow of energy even more and bring euphoric pleasure to the entire body and emotions.

ET Visitations

There has been a lot of attention in the media in the past few years regarding galactic spacecraft visiting Earth. For nearly a century people have reported seeing unidentified flying objects, and have shared encounters in which they were taken on board by aliens for some scientific purpose. I believe it is wise to entertain the idea that we are not alone in the universe and that we are not the only conscious or intellectual beings in our galaxy. My hope is that when our galactic family does make their presence known, our military does not attempt to blast them with nuclear weapons. Whatever we do to our planet affects every star, planet, galaxy, and consciousness in our universe—and possibly beyond. Starseeds come to serve both Earth and their own world, according to the Universe's plan of unity.

I have never had a visitation by an ET (extraterrestrial) but I know a woman whose body has held various ET walk-ins who stay for a specific purpose and then depart. She possesses knowledge and wisdom beyond this world, and the energy that she carries is like no other I have ever experienced. I was spiritually activated and received downloads the entire time she and I were together. After sitting with her group in meditation, I was convinced that she is indeed working with aspects of galactic consciousness. While ET visitations are phenomenal and galactic beings can and do incarnate into human bodies, not all visitations result in a walk-in event or soul exchange.

Near-Death Experience

Since I wrote about near-death experiences in my book, *More Than Meets the Eye ~ True Stories about Death, Dying, and Afterlife*, I will not go into a lot of detail about it here. Life reviews, traveling through a tunnel of light, meeting deceased loved ones, Jesus, and other ascended masters, being told to go back and complete this lifetime— are included in the reports we hear when a person's soul temporarily visits the afterlife and returns to the body. This can easily facilitate a pre-arranged soul swap, but not everyone who has a near-death experience is a walk-in.

Channeling

Many people can channel entities, and everyone can receive messages from their spirit guides. Some channels surrender their bodies to the entity who wants to speak through them. I have never been a fan of giving up that kind of control, but I have received some powerful messages while in a self-induced trance-like state. It is unlikely that a soul exchange would occur through channeling, but I am not limiting my beliefs to say that it could not happen.

Mid-life Crisis or Dark Night of the Soul

My walk-in occurred while I was in the darkest, saddest, and most upsetting time of my life. I was forty years old and experiencing several simultaneous emotionally challenging events when I lost the will to live. I just wanted to be free of the sorrow of Earth life and go home. Little did I know that these events set up the circumstances for the walk-in that my natal soul had agreed to prior to incarnation.

There is no need to create chaos in order to walk out. Therefore, not everyone who goes through a dark night of the soul or mid-life crisis will encounter a soul exchange, but many walk-outs/walk-ins have used times of distress as an exit/entry point. A highly-evolved soul may consciously facilitate a soul swap or soul merge as directed by the monad (intelligence hub of your soul group) in order to support the new world of crystalline energy.

Chapter 4 ~ How to Tell If You are a Walk-in

The first soul to reside in my body knew it was in for a hard trip—it seems that part of the plan was to make sure her life experiences would carry her through an emotional meat grinder. With multiple surgeries, illnesses, and injuries, the physical body got pretty banged up as well. Thankfully, there was a backup plan—a soul exchange would occur when the ride got too rough and the natal soul wanted off the merry-go-round. It was agreed that another soul would step in when the natal soul reached a point in which she gave up on life. A two-year period of depression indicated that she was ready to leave and experience the soul exchange.

When I was receiving energy work from Roni Angel (Doctor of Psychology and creator of CHORD Therapy), I gave her a copy of my first book, *Email Episodes ~ A Hilariously Honest Look at Life.* She immediately recognized that I was a walk-in, but she did not mention it to me right away. (We walk-ins tend to recognize one another.) As Roni and I were talking, she shared her personal walk-in story. My mouth dropped open, I felt like I was going to burst into tears, and I could hardly speak. I asked her if she thought I might be a walk-in, and she said that I had many indications to suggest that probability. I had never heard of such a thing as a walk-in. I had many times thought that I had died and come back alive in the same body.

After that revelation, I began to process the karmic imprint of the old soul, and clear away the "brain damage" of the first forty years of my very religious life. That is when my writing career took wings. Soon, I began to step into my new role as an author and teacher, and later as a coach for empaths and walk-ins.

Some individuals who come to me for coaching think they may be a walk-in, but are not sure. While there is no proof other than what your own heart tells you, there are some similarities that seem to indicate such an experience.

Indications That a Walk-In Has Occurred

- An abrupt change in personality that may have resulted from a dissociative event, near-death experience, suicide attempt, or other perilous marker.
- Feeling like your body has been short circuited or that your nerves have been fried.
- Feeling that you are a stranger in your own body
- Brain fog or sudden loss of memory.
- Having a sense that you are a misfit on Earth. This feeling may have intensified when the two souls swapped places.
- Suddenly having chronic fatigue and muscle pain such as fibromyalgia. For me, this started with the actual event that pinned me to the floor, and lasted for more than two years afterward.
- Spiritual gifts suddenly opening up: You start to know things about people that no one has told you. You suddenly start to see, hear, or feel non-physical beings around you. You become more telepathic. Your sensitivity to energy increases. You touch someone and they are healed.

Quiz for Determining If You Are a Walk-in

Take a moment to write down your answers on another sheet of paper. It can help you determine if and when you walked into the body you are now in. Knowing the date will be very important when you have your walk-in astrology chart done. Maxine Taylor, who specializes in reading charts for walk-ins, can help you with this. Maxine is CNN's former on-air astrologer, a national speaker, and a co-founder of the Atlanta Astrological Society, the Atlanta Board of Astrology Examiners and the Atlanta Institute of Metaphysics. She currently serves on the Board of Directors of the American Federation of Astrologers.

- When you first had a spiritually-transforming experience, what emotional or physical changes did you notice about yourself?

- What was different about your thinking patterns? Was there a thought or phrase that was repeated?

- Did your body seem strange or new, as if it did not belong to you?

- What were the circumstances of your life just prior to the event that caused you to suspect that you are a walk-in?

- Did you have a lapse of memory regarding your childhood?

- Were there significant life alterations, such as career changes, a miraculous physical healing, an urge to end a relationship, dress differently, redecorate, or relocate?

- Was there a shift in your beliefs and life values after this significant event?

- If you have had more than one walk-in experience were there common signs that you now recognize that indicated you were about to shift?

- Did you notice a change in your spirit guides or your ability to receive spiritual guidance?

- What has been the most challenging thing about integrating the higher vibrating energy of your walk-in soul?

Muscle Testing

This does not work for everyone, but there has been a lot of research showing the validity of muscle testing. You can use this test whenever you have a spiritual question and you need a true or false answer. Kinesiology also helps us with selecting the food and supplements we need to support our bodies.

Before doing this exercise, it is important to center your energy and come to a still point inside your personal space. Take a few deep breaths and sense whatever is going on for you at that moment—feel the seat you are sitting on, notice the smells and sounds around you, the feelings in your body. See/feel yourself letting go and dropping any energy that does not belong to you. Then, call your own energy back from wherever it might have wandered, passing it through the ultraviolet flame of transmutation as it returns to your field/body. This can help bring you into the now moment or still point where you are ready to hear from your higher self.

Now, with your index finger and thumb on each hand, form a circle. Connect the finger circles together like links on a chain and pull tight. The resistance you feel should be strong. Make a false statement, such as "My name is Elmer Fudd" and try to pull the links apart. Now, unless your name really is Elmer Fudd, that connection probably weakened and you were able to pull the circles apart quite easily. Your muscles will typically weaken in response to a false statement.

Now, reconnect the finger circles and state your real name: "My name is _____." Most likely your link stayed strong. This indicates that your body perceives this as a true statement.

Next, state to yourself, "I am a walk-in," and try to pull the finger circles apart. If you are a walk-in, your body perceives this statement as true and you probably were not able to break the link. If you are not a walk-in, then you will probably be able to break the connection very easily.

Feel free to share the results of your tests on our Facebook page: http://www.facebook.com/WalkInEvolution.

Chapter 5 ~ My Walk-in Story

Prior to my walk-in in 1999, I was under a lot of emotional stress due to many changes in my life that occurred over a relatively short time. My family and I had lived in four houses in three different states in less than five years. My marriage was going under, my son had graduated from high school and left home, my daughter had gotten extremely sick and was hospitalized, and I had lost the leadership positions that I had enjoyed in every church we had attended.

My first husband and I had an argument three weeks after we were married. He left during our "discussion," and even though he returned once he had processed his feelings, I began stuffing my true thoughts and feelings from that day forward. Our church taught that wives were to obey their husbands without question, and that is what I did for the next two decades.

The second argument we had was twenty-two years later on December 3, 1999. As an obedient wife, I had stuffed my true feelings and had never challenged him on any issue. Yet, for almost a year at that point, I had begun to stand up for myself. I had established a friendship with several women (a first for me) at a three-day retreat that I attended on how to heal from abuse and emotional trauma. I went to see a movie with a girlfriend one Friday night. When I returned about 10 p.m., my husband met me at the top of the garage stairs and wanted to know where I had been. I was puzzled by this because he had known where I was going before I left. We got into an argument, which traumatized me so much that I passed out and fell to the floor. He tried to rouse me and when he could not, he panicked and called the counselor I had been seeing. My daughter, who was sixteen at the time, came running to the bedroom to see what was going on. I could hear her and my husband talking to me and to one another, but I could not speak, nor could I get my body to move or get up. At first, I thought this was an episode of being "slain in the Spirit"—a phenomenon I had experienced in the Pentecostal churches we had attended, but this was different. I felt paralyzed and frightened until I heard a calm, soothing internal voice say, "Relax. This is for your own good. You will understand later." I felt peace wash over me as I laid there for about ten minutes.

When that dissociative episode ended and I was able to arise, I felt strangely different. I felt empowered! I put on my nightgown and got ready for bed. I was not about to sleep with this man who had triggered such an episode, or risk another traumatic event, so I went upstairs and slept in the room that had been my son's before he moved out on his own. Needless to say, I did not sleep at all that night. Angels constantly ministered to me with a sweet adoring presence that was so tangible it felt like someone was actually touching me or wrapping my body in a warm blanket of love.

The next morning, I packed my bags and left home. I felt so disoriented that I forgot to tell my daughter goodbye. I did not even call my mom or tell anyone where I was going. I did not know where I was going! I ended up at the house of one of the women I had met at the retreat. The next day, I paid for a week's stay at the Economy Inn. I had some of the most comforting, vivid and lucid dreams that week, which gave me the confidence I needed to start my new life as a single woman.

Even though I still loved them, I felt like I did not know my own children or mother. My daughter started asking what was wrong with me and saying things like, "You are not the same person you used to be—you are so different!" I felt so strange over the next few months, as if I were watching myself do things that I had never had the courage to do before. I was creating all kinds of change. For example, I needed full-time employment with benefits rather than the part-time position I had had while I was married, so I signed up with a temporary agency while I searched for something more permanent. I had played keyboards for hours each day for the thirty years prior, but within a year of my walk-in, I stopped playing music of any kind.

The members of the church I was attending at the time harshly judged me for leaving my marriage. So, I stopped going to church. However, I had an urge to investigate a particular office park every time I drove past it. I was disappointed to find a church that was meeting in a warehouse in the very back of the complex. I was on auto-pilot and not fully present in any of the decisions I was making, but I knew my guidance wanted me to go to that church. I later understood that my zombie-like condition was normal. The natal soul was observing (and sometimes appalled by) the changes being made by the walk-in soul who was now in charge. I procrastinated in attending that church for several weeks until I was unable to ignore the relentless urging that persisted even when I was not in that area of town. I reluctantly showed up on Easter Sunday in 2000 and met a man there who became my husband ten weeks later. My natal soul would never have made such a hasty decision.

During that time, I kept thinking to myself that I had died and come back to life as another person. I didn't even believe in reincarnation at the time, so even entertaining that idea was a stretch of the imagination. I had had a near-death experience before, but the change it created afterward was nothing like the transformation following the dissociative episode in my bedroom that December night.

I noticed that my childhood memories had been swept clean from my mind. Other than some vague snippets of an abusive event with a babysitter when I was about five years old (I repressed the memory of that abuse for thirty-five years), I completely drew a blank when I tried to envision anything about my life as a child. My mom helped me fill in the blanks of my childhood and slowly more memories came back as I looked through family photo albums. On top of that, my nerves were on edge and it took several years for my nervous system to repair itself as I acclimated to the higher frequencies of the walk-in soul. I had terrible pain in my neck, shoulders, and upper back, which felt like I had been stabbed or had some invisible "wings" ripped from my back. I was diagnosed with fibromyalgia, but all this pain went away within a couple of years.

All these abrupt changes in my behavior made some people think that I was having a nervous breakdown. I was working part-time for a drug and alcohol abuse counselor when my walk-in occurred. When he saw the dissociation episodes I was having, he wanted to put me in a treatment facility. While I would have enjoyed a two-week stay somewhere safe and away from the pressures of everyday life, I knew that if I went into treatment I would carry that record with me the rest of my life. I did not know why I was experiencing such peculiar things, but I absolutely knew I was not mentally ill. Some well-meaning people were actually harming my fragile condition by stressing me out with their expectations that I perform as if nothing had happened. I pulled away from them and started my own self-treatment plan, and simply began to love myself unconditionally through whatever hell or high water I found myself in.

I remembered what I had heard when I was pinned to the floor: You will understand later. My research to discover what was happening to me began after Roni Angel shared her walk-in experience with me, but there was little material on the topic other than what I found at Healpastlives.com. (Some years later I read Ruth Montgomery's book, *Strangers Among Us*.) Armed with the new information I had, life started to make sense even though this walk-in idea was far removed from what I had believed was possible—especially since I came from a very religious background.

One day, I decided to accept and allow myself to be at peace with the idea that perhaps I was a walk-in. As I owned this as my truth, my emotions calmed down and I accepted the many changes I had created in my new life.

My walk-in was a harrowing experience that totally changed my life. It was a true soul exchange. However, I had another experience in 2005 that was like a second installment of the walk-in soul's energy. I think that if the full supply of higher dimensional energy had come in during the 1999 walk-in, it would have damaged my nervous system beyond repair.

I knew that something spiritual was about to occur when I was diagnosed as having a tumor in my colon. Even though the doctor thought it was likely malignant, I had no fear about the surgery I was facing. Instead, I grieved because it felt like I was going away, and I did not want to leave the wonderful family I had walked into. It was not until later that I realized that it was not the walk-in soul who was leaving; my natal soul was detaching from my auric field where she had been an observer for five years since the soul exchange.

My guides had told me beforehand that the surgery was being used to facilitate a spiritual experience, and that my body would in no way suffer harm. When I awoke in recovery, I felt totally peaceful, and sensed angels and guides all around me. I heard their comforting words as they instructed me to breathe deeply. It is hard to explain how or why that surgery was a pleasant experience for my body and soul, but I had very little pain or discomfort and I was at peace before, during, and afterward. I went home twenty-four hours after surgery, much to the surprise of my doctors. I was supposed to have been in the hospital for three to five days. I stayed in a state of bliss for about two months thereafter.

I have experienced several downloads of higher energy, had a visitation by an oversoul (one of the souls in a monad group or soul matrix), integrated a future self, and processed DNA code activations since then. Each one is easier to integrate and the results are always good.

Chapter 6 ~ Stories from Other Walk-ins

In the 1980s and 1990s there was an explosion of consciousness on the planet, and the walk-in phenomenon was very real for a lot of people. This explosion of consciousness burst open doors and suddenly there were reports of out-of-body and near-death experiences, walk-ins, ET visitations, and UFO sightings. Some called these experiences "spiritual awakenings" or "psychic breakthroughs." Yet, some psychologists and therapists called them "breakdowns." When someone had a walk-in experience back then he or she may have felt very much alone.

If you were going to a therapist at that time and said you were having weird experiences, they would have called it "dissociation." That is the therapeutic term, but in our metaphysical and spiritual world we call it expanded consciousness or extraordinary consciousness. Over the past twenty years, we have come to realize that this phenomenon is not as rare as you might think. There were so many reported experiences of extraordinary consciousness or expanded awareness during this time that the psychiatric profession looked for help from therapists who were studying metaphysics and physics at that time in Stamford, Connecticut and New York.

These experiences helped prepare us for our current days of enhanced spirituality and increased vibration. I believe walk-ins are here to help develop multidimensional awareness and oneness (non-polarized) consciousness. We have the ability to change planetary frequencies through our own vibrational attunements and upgrades.

A walk-in experience is a term used by Ruth Montgomery, a journalist who loved metaphysics and began a writing career by doing journalistic research. When she ran into Carol Parish-Harra, who is one of the first walk-ins mentioned in her book, she began to investigate others. So Ruth was the person everybody called when they had this kind of experience.

If you look into the harmonic convergence in 1987, and the energy leading up to it, you will find Liz Montgomery, a woman who founded Walk-ins for Evolutions (known as WE International, LLC). This group opened conversation, allowed people to meet and share socially, and gain understanding from others. Hundreds of people gathered in the mid- to late-1990s for several conferences about how to adjust to the walk-in shift. It was very helpful to know that others had undergone the same phenomenon.

Many years have passed, decades in fact, but this organization is still active thanks to a walk-in named Ranoli. She was an original member of the group and maintained the organization for many years after Liz passed from her body. The week before Thanksgiving 2012, I was driving to my parent's house in Georgia when I felt a strong prompting to call Ranoli and accept the presidency of WE International, LLC. She had offered me the position in 2011, but I did not feel the time was right then. Ranoli was elated to have someone relieve her of the burden she had been carrying while also recovering from cancer. As the president of WE, I plan to organize online courses, interactive conference calls, and in-person gatherings to see Liz's original vision fulfilled.

One thing that the WE International conferences offered was an opportunity for walk-ins to share their personal stories. I have included a few in this chapter. I also want to offer you a chance to share yours on our blog walkinevolution.blogspot.com.

Armine's Story

Armine's walk-in did not take place in one event or on one particular day, but rather over a period of time. Her full awakening started in May or June of 2011, but the process began in 1999 when she lost her dad. After witnessing his treatment in a traditional, fear-based medical setting, she started reading books, subscribing to alternative care magazines, and stopped going to doctors. She relied on home remedies and completely changed her lifestyle. In 2002, she found a lump in her throat and was in a lot of discomfort. She felt that she did not have any choice but to go to a doctor.

The doctor did not know what the lump could be. He wanted to admit her to a hospital to look into her throat through a scope, get a biopsy, and run tests. She refused to be a guinea pig and declined that type of treatment. Armine heard about a man who works from his home doing a lot of energy therapy for cancer patients, so she called him the next day and got an appointment. He never gave her a diagnosis or a label, but within five sessions, the lump was gone, she felt great, and she was back to normal. He became her doctor from then on and she went to him for years—many times he would check her energy over the phone and tell her what to do to heal.

Armine met a Reiki practitioner, a woman that she saw for medical or emotional problems over the years, who does not speak English well. Seva is Turkish and speaks Russian—they always had difficulty communicating with each other if Seva's son or daughter was not there to translate. She has a group that meditates together to heal our planet. She also teaches students who are interested in energy, keeping chakras clear, and how to meditate. In one class that Armine attended, Seva took the class on a journey to meet their spirit guides. Armine was accompanied through a dark tunnel at the end of which was a bright light. She went through the light and saw a door that opened automatically. She entered a room. On the left side was a garden. Armine said, "Whoever my guides are, I am inviting you here." A light came to her, and she very briefly saw a face. Armine grew up in a communist country and was never exposed to God or Jesus; therefore, she was completely unaware of spiritual ideas or Bible stories. But, all of a sudden she saw Jesus' face; he was a smiling, bubbly young man with long shoulder-length blond hair, and he was wearing a black polo shirt.

"What is your name?" she asked.

"Chris," he replied.

"Oh, my God! Chris, I did not know you were my guide." She was crying.

He said, "I just want to let you know that everything is going to be just fine in your life." Then he gave Armine her cosmic code—a personal password that we are all assigned at birth—like one might use to log into a computer.

"What do I do with this code?"

"You can come back anytime you want or if you have any questions. Simply come here and say that password and one of your guides will come," he replied.

She did not know that we could have more than one guide.

After that, she went back several times, and she met other guides, including a young man from Madrid, Spain. She started meditating every day, opening her chakras and cleaning her aura. She and her guides became good friends, and she would chat with them every day, asking millions of questions. One day, she asked them if they saw her dad. They said no, which confused her. "If they are spirits," she said, "they should know my dad."

One Sunday morning, Armine was at her kitchen counter making a salad, when all of a sudden, a clear vision came to her. She saw her dad in a holographic way. She put everything down and said "Dad, it's you!" She started crying. "I am sorry I have not been at your gravesite for such a long time."

"No, no, no! Do not worry; I am not dead."

She was doubting herself, thinking it was her imagination. Her dad spoke, read, and wrote in fluent Russian, a language that he loved. He regretted that his wife and children never knew how to speak it.

"Dad," she said, "Do you still speak Russian?"

"Yes, sometimes I speak Russian with Yasha."

When she heard that name she knew it could not have been her imagination. Yasha was her dad's friend when Armine was a little girl. He would come to their house to spend time with her Dad. She had not heard or remembered this name for more than forty years.

Her dad was a big-time meat eater; he especially loved to eat beef. "Dad, is there food where you are?" she asked.

"We only have fruits here," he said. "Stop eating meat. It is not good for you."

Armine stopped eating animal protein that very day.

At the time, she was going through menopause and was on bio-identical hormones so she asked her dad if these were really natural. He said, "Yes, most of them are natural. When they compound them, they add some chemicals to make them into a cream form."

"How long should I use these?"

"When the right time comes, the message will come to you clearly." About ten months later, she received a letter from her holistic doctor, saying she was closing down her practice. At first she worried about how she was going to find another doctor whom she loved as much as this one. She had built a close relationship with this doctor and was not ready to see someone new. But then she realized that this was the message that it was time to stop the bio-identical hormones. She called her doctor to ask if she would experience withdrawal. She was told that they were all natural and that she could stop any time. If any symptoms come back, she could start taking them again. The symptoms did not come back because she kept her vibration high.

In another meditation, she began to see a very pure and angelic girl who looked just like her, only a younger version. Her clothes were the style that women wore in the 1940s or 1950s. She had a black bobbed wavy hairstyle, the same as Armine did in her younger years.

"Who are you?" she asked.

"My name is Maria."

"You look just like me!"

"Yes, and I watch you every day," said Maria.

"Is there anything you want to tell me?"

"No, not right now." She faded away.

Later that day, she was conversing with her guides and mentioned that she had met this girl during meditation. They affirmed that Maria had come from Eastern Europe and was one of the spirits on her guidance team.

"Are you ever going to come back to life?" Armine asked her guides.

"Yes."

"When? Where?"

"We are helping you now so we can come back to Earth life. When you reach your goal, we are going to reincarnate."

"Are you going to come back as a baby?"

"No, we are going to continue our lives where we left off," Chris said.

"Are you going to come back as a thirty-something-year-old?"

"Yes. And we will choose someone who has the same physical features and appearance as we do."

"How is that possible?"

"Every day on this planet, people like you wake up. When they wake up, spirits like us enter their body."

"Am I ever going to see you in a body?"

"Yes."

"You have to promise me that you will make an appearance to me. I want to see you in your physical life."

"You will, I promise."

Then, she began to worry that if they came back, they would not be her guides anymore. She had built a great friendship with them even though they were invisible. "What am I going to do if I do not have you?" she asked.

"Do not worry. When you reach your goal, you are not going to need our help."

"What do you mean? I need guides. If you cannot be my guides then I choose Maria to be my guide."

"Yeah, you can do that. She can replace us."

On August 29, 2011, Armine awoke with a sensation that felt like a volcano was erupting in her head. Confused and foggy-headed, she did not understand what was going on. She realized that whatever questions she had that day would not be answered by her guides. In fact, she never saw them again. She was connected to some new source or field of information and did not have to ask questions. Answers seemed to come from thin air.

A couple of days later she started arising between 3 and 4 a.m., the purest communication time. She asked, "Where are my angels and guides?"

"They came back to physical life," she heard.

"Am I going to meet them?"

Immediately a vision began. There was an auditorium where a lot of people were gathered. "You are going to see them and meet them at one of these gatherings."

"Where is Maria?"

"Maria is *in* you."

Armine started crying.

During the integration stage of her walk-in, Armine went to her Reiki master because she continued to be so emotional. The Reiki master did a private channeling and let her know that Maria was from Sirius. Many walk-in souls come from Sirius or Pleiades and have been Native American Indians in past lives.

After her walk-in Armine started doing things that she had never done before. She started doing yoga every day, began completely taking care of her body, and joined a Reiki masters group that meditated with an emphasis on healing the planet. All twenty-five women were Russian, and spoke both Russian and English. However, the leader spoke fluent Russian and very poor English, which meant Armine could not communicate with her. She had to sit next to someone who could translate for her. One Saturday, she was driving to work and hearing chatter in her mind. This time it was in Russian and she was able to understand it. "What is going on with me? I talk Russian now?" she said. She was so shocked by this revelation that she pulled her car off the road.

When she arrived at work, she found her co-worker, who speaks fluent Russian, and said to her in Russian, "Talk Russian to me because now I can speak it."

"What is going on with you? I am going to faint now," the co-worker laughed. "It's impossible. I mean, you knew words here and there, but you never spoke it like you just did."

Armine picked up the phone, called Seva, and started talking to her in Russian. Even though this surprised her, Seva knew that Armine's dad had given her this gift of language so she could meditate with the group to help heal the planet. The group was shocked that she could suddenly communicate and totally understand what everyone in the group was talking about. She no longer needed anyone to translate for her, which helped her feel much more connected to the group and the planet.

Little by little she built a great online spiritual community and became a translator for galacticchannelings.com. They have thirty-eight languages into which spirit messages are translated. She translates them into her native Armenian language. She has also participated in a spirituality show called *In Light Radio*.

Armine is now connected with an extraterrestrial who told her she had a lot more projects coming. Many of them would be done through her dream state, but there are also physical projects for her. In August 2012, she helped with the YouTube video, "I Know My Galactic Family Is Here."

The natal soul is no longer in her body. Everyday problems no longer bother her. If she has an off day, she bounces right back. She meditates to connect with the Earth, animals, and all the living things. If she senses agitation she goes within herself to feel at peace and know that things are always good. If her kids forget to call, she no longer panics as she did before her walk-in. She trusts that they are all fine, and then within a minute or two they call her.

All the things she has experienced and participated in, all the steps she has taken to heal, all these benevolent things are because of the soul exchange, a pre-birth contract she agreed to.

Armine said, "We have untapped sources of energy and knowledge and we are now bringing all the gifts from all our lifetimes into this current lifetime."

Mary

About the time I was finishing up this book, a friend that I had known since my church days in Indiana contacted me on Facebook. We had not been in touch for seven years. I had changed a lot since the last time we had seen one another, but there was also something different about Mary and her vibration. She was happy and excited even though she had just ended a meaningful relationship a few months prior.

As we were talking, I began to feel an overload of energy, and my head started pounding. This is common for me when I am submersed in intense energy for several hours; however, we had only been together for twenty or so minutes. I laid my head on the table and stabilized my energy field as she began to tell me about an experience she had had two weeks prior.

She was asleep in bed when she began to feel an intense presence walk into the room and move toward her. She looked over her shoulder to see if someone was there, but she saw nothing unusual. The next thing she knew she was pinned down and could not move or speak. Her initial reaction was fear, and she remembered the King James Bible stating that people were "sore afraid" when visited angels. She assumed this was an angel, and while she wasn't exactly panicking, she did feel uneasy that she could smother while unable to lift her head from the pillow. She surrendered to whatever was happening and trusted that if she did die, her soul would be fine.

Once she was able to move, she felt strangely different. Her intuition was keener, and she started seeing people in visions before seeing them in person; she now hears her internal guidance very clearly, and synchronicities have become a daily experience. She also acquired an urge to start connecting with the local spiritual community.

She had never heard of a walk-in, but when I told her about my experience, it resonated with her. She had a strong sensation that a soul shift or walk-in had occurred for her. Having that information brought peace because it helped her know that she wasn't crazy since many everyday people are having strange experiences like hers. Mary says she feels more alive, whole, and hopeful than ever in her life!

Ranoli

This next story is from Ranoli, an original member of WE International who became the president, and kept the organization alive after Liz Nelson passed from her body.

Ranoli remembers waking up or coming to, so to speak, on the floor of a motel. She looked at her hand and thought, "Fingers . . . hand," and then flexing the fingers and thinking, "Okay, this is how you make the hand work." And then she thought, "Oh hell, I am in this body and it is tight!

The awareness came slowly and then very swiftly. It took some time to get her body up off of the floor... She stumbled about for a bit, not really having control of her body. When she sat up on the bed, she was very surprised—scared, actually—that it moved. She used her brain much as we would use a computer, pulling up files and finding information to tell her why the bed moved. Ah, a waterbed, of course.

This all started July 5, 1985. Her body was thirty years old, but her soul had not been in physical form on Earth for over 10,000 years when Atlantis was in the process of being destroyed. She remembered that lifetime so clearly—she was a walk-in then, as well.

She recalled with great clarity the "before" time, when she was still free in form and not contained in a body. She was sitting at a computer-like machine, though it was not like any technology that is currently on this planet. This machine allowed energy vibrations to be calculated to determine how the balance of light and darkness were being held; it held and grounded energies that were being fed to this plane, which enabled growth, peace, and balance. Ranoli is a galactic ambassador, teaching worlds and civilizations how to balance the polarities of light and dark and their many forms. So, for Ranoli, Earth is an experience of polarity integration.

Her last memories before selecting this life experience were of being in a galactic battle. As an ambassador traveling to other worlds, she would sometimes be aboard a type of spaceship that has a very special relationship with an organic humanoid-type being. The ship itself is known as an Ashtar, and the fleet is known as the Ashtar Command. She was traveling aboard one of these ships going to the Alpha Draconian star system for a meeting with representatives from other planets. They were working on freeing a civilization from slavery. The humanoid aspect of the Ashtar ship in which Ranoli traveled was defecting and setting up all of the ambassadors attending this meeting for capture by a rogue group in the Alpha Draconian system.

Ranoli knew this, and warned the other ambassadors and the galactic federation. A battle ensued between the rogue Draconians and the loyal Ashtar ships. Ranoli was sent to Earth to save her soul from being vaporized. On Earth, we believe souls cannot be destroyed, but Ranoli's memories tell her otherwise.

Ranoli is an energy consultant, who brings in and holds energies to help raise consciousness. In some cases, she removes energy to allow higher consciousness to develop. Coming to Earth was a natural choice as her skills were needed here and this was a safe place for her to be.

As she was preparing for this life experience, she recalls standing in front of a big screen, working out the details of this life, just as souls do before descending into physical form. There were many other beings around, who specialize in this type of work: the guiding of life choice.

Ranoli also remembers having a conversation with her walk-out, agreeing together that they would trade places. She would assume responsibility for the natal soul's contracts and core life lessons, and complete them to the very best of her ability while also completing her own work.

She remembers the feeling of excitement, love, and joy because many of her comrades were coming in to fulfill a mission that was needed to balance the energies. There were screens with many excited groups waiting for the final movement that would place them into a physical body. There were many souls going many places, some to other dimensions, other planets, and some to Earth. Some would walk into adult bodies and some would walk into newborn bodies.

When her time to walk in arrived, she saw her body on the floor of the motel room and knew that it was time for her to enter. Many beings were there to help with the process. Some were there to protect, some to do meta-surgery of a sort, others to help connect her soul to the body.

She saw her walk-out leaving and severing the silver cord that connected her to the body; and then the meta-surgeons connected a silver cord from Ranoli's energy field to the physical body, and helped her re-animate the body. It is true that for just a moment, the walk-in's body is dead, without a consciousness, and that is why protection is needed while the two souls exchange places.

Since being here, Ranoli has come to realize that Earth is a mystery, and she does not understand much that happens here. Because of that, she has had many experiences to help her understand the choices humans make and why. These life experiences helped her feel and understand the human condition. For Ranoli, that meant becoming very ill and having accidents to knock issues loose. She agrees that many walk-ins have to clear health issues, and clear out the emotional baggage of the walk-outs. The walk-in cannot move forward into their own work until that is complete. Like many beings, once Ranoli arrived and found out what Earth life was all about, she wanted to leave. She was subconsciously giving her body a message to shut down (the death wish) so she could leave. Her body did exactly that and she became very ill.

During a severe illness, she knew that if she woke up, she would survive the illness, but she could just as easily leave. In that moment, she knew that it was okay to leave, to die. She was not afraid of dying, but she had not accomplished what she came here to do and for that reason, she chose to stay. It was at that point that she realized the messages she was giving her body, and how powerful her words and thoughts were. Things shifted immediately after that. Her words, thoughts, feelings, and actions began to reflect her desire to be on Earth, to complete her work/mission, and to have fun doing it. She no longer saw Earth as alien or foreign. She belonged here and knew it. At that point, she fully entered into her body and liked it. That was very powerful and healing for her.

Ranoli says, "I think many of us walk away from the responsibility of doing the healing work necessary to make the body our own and then to fully enter into it. We do not understand the value of clearing the emotional issues. We can only do our work cleanly if we are clear vessels and that means clearing the emotional body.

"For many walk-ins, the emotional body makes no sense. We understand the love aspects, but the fear aspects are a mystery to us and confuse us. I am sure that is the truth for many "born-ins," as we all come from someplace else and many of those places do not have emotional bodies.

In order for Ranoli to understand love on this plane, she had to understand all the conditions, pain, and fears humans place on love. By having those experiences, she came to understand love as it is experienced by humans on this plane. Because of that understanding she can now do the work she has come here to do: teach a new method by which to experience relationship. She calls this "soul-driven relationship" verses "ego-driven relationship." There is no model for this type of relating on earth yet, but it is possible for this paradigm to be expressed. Many individuals are choosing to live life consciously, meaning that we are making choices as to how we will live our lives and how we will relate to others.

Ranoli noticed how willing humans are to give up their power and follow someone else's truth, whether it feels right for them or not. They blindly believe what others say. It makes no sense to Ranoli why individuals do not want to own their power, to be self-responsible, to grasp their knowingness, and to live their lives by that knowledge.

She says, "It is through our personal truth that the power to transform this world lies. If we are reluctant to find and use that knowingness and the gifts that come with it, then we can never complete our personal missions. We did not come here to be clones, but to be individuals expressing our own truth. By expressing our own truth and being true to our soul expression, we grow and learn; we experience our own creation. Many of us try to do this from outside of our bodies; we do not want to be present in the moment within our bodies. If we could have completed our work from outside of a human body there would have been no need for us to come here. We could simply have done whatever we came to do from out there, wherever 'out there' is."

Had someone shared with her, when she first arrived, how to integrate, work through emotional issues, and make her life and body her own, it would have saved her much pain. But, she might not have learned all the things she needed to learn through that pain. Had she missed the victim stage that is so core to the human experience, she might not have remembered that everything that happens in life is her own creation.

"We are not victims," says Ranoli. "We create everything that happens to us. We are masters at creating, so take responsibility for what you have created; view it, change what you feel is outdated, and create something new that reflects who you are today. Make those creations based on what you know as truth, not what someone else tells you is true."

Brenda Williams & Morgan

Brenda Williams was raising her children when she became physically debilitated and was diagnosed with terminal cancer in 1990. There was no prior indication that anything was out of the ordinary until she found a lump while taking a shower. A quick phone call to the doctor set up an immediate appointment to check it out. Dr. Parker called later that evening to tell Brenda that he had her surgery scheduled for 7:30 a.m. the next morning to have her breast and the lump removed. The surgery revealed a lot of lymph node involvement with an aggressive DNA marker.

Her team of doctors decided to do a very potent chemo treatment that might prolong her life for six months. Her husband was frantic, and everyone wanted her to do whatever she had to do to live a little longer, but she knew it was not going to work. Brenda went to the first treatment and had such bizarre side effects that she refused additional treatments. She said that if she was going to die of cancer, she would rather die with hair on her head rather than with her head over the toilet!

Her oncologist asked her to stay in touch with him frequently, even though she would receive no further treatment. While everyone was waiting for her to die, she began to have an awareness—a knowing that was quite alien to her. So, she began to journal every experience and write about the conversations she was having with spirit beings from higher realms.

As she sat outside on her deck every day, she began to experience a difference in rhythms as she noticed birds coming to the feeder, wind blowing in the trees, and the movement of nature around her. The next thing she knew her sensory system had become quite keen. Brenda started to feel better as she disregarded some of the fearful stuff that was going on. She began to have a few flashback memories that were a little scary so she talked to a physician friend, who was also a psychologist. During one of the flashbacks, she asked if he would do hypnosis to get a better idea of what was going on. Under hypnosis, she had full recollection of an indigenous lifestyle. The doctor figured Brenda was making up a really clever story, but he decided to do some research. That is when he discovered that her facts perfectly described an authentic tribe.

Within the year, she flipped back into the old fear-based patterns and found another lump. However, the biopsy results that showed it was benign. Two weeks later, she found another lump, which was borderline. Even though her bone scan was clean, she and her surgeon determined it would be best to remove the other breast and continue the reconstruction process. This gave her the alone time she needed to allow this new reality to be better understood.

When her husband passed away in 2000, Brenda sold her house and became fully engaged with her companion walk-in, Morgan Trent, who is a future version of herself. Morgan has come in and out bringing an enormous amount of information regarding the technical work they are doing together.

In 2008, Brenda was pronounced dead in a hospice—not from cancer but from something else. She was shown from the other side that she and Morgan would switch places. Rather than having Brenda in the body one day and Morgan in it the next, the process to embody Morgan's essence required Brenda and Morgan to work closely together to ensure a seamless collaboration. This process allowed Morgan's consciousness to become very fluid within Brenda's form. That part was not difficult. The complexities came when it was time for Morgan to become fully acquainted with being in form. The cosmic aspect of us has no idea of how to work with emotions. Therefore, Morgan was constantly in a state of frustration, annoyance, and impatience asking, "What's the matter with you people? What do you mean you do not understand what I am saying?" Morgan has learned to be playful and is assimilating well now. Looking at pictures of herself over the years, Brenda can tell when Morgan has been in the lead because her hair is cut short and there is a difference in the cadence of her voice.

Until late 2012, not even her family or closest friends knew her story. Some of the people that she worked with knew bits and pieces of it, but the part that had to do with how the Earth Brenda and the cosmic Brenda (or future Morgan) would swap places was so unusual that she kept it private.

When Brenda talks she rarely knows what is going to come out of her mouth; it all depends on the vibrational frequency of the group. The whole story came out in a small group setting one Tuesday night in late 2012. She was packed and ready to leave for a conference on the west coast the next day. That morning, Morgan's presence was much more in Brenda's body than she had been previously, and she was not going anywhere this time. She brought her luggage and her own special coffee cup! About three o'clock that Tuesday afternoon, she pulled down a flipchart and started to write some notes to share with the group. As usual, she was surprised by what started flowing. "These people are going to freak out when I start to babble all this stuff!" she said. "This is crazy! I am heading up there to expose myself!"

Then she heard, "It is time. Do it in a way so people will see that it is not a big deal."

Typically, Brenda would hold back, but this time Morgan was fully engaged and the presentation flowed with ease. She did not hold back a single part of her story.

Over the years, Brenda came to understand how the body works with consciousness and how the body heals itself. Part of Brenda's purpose for being on the planet is to share information about how two soul aspects can come together and share a body. It is important for our cosmic wisdom to be anchored in the physical form so our evolved souls (future selves) can work by being on the planet. We are all going to have similar experiences because we are all merging into our higher forms. Many walk-ins today are in collaboration with beings in multi-verses. While this is the first time the human population has had this opportunity, it will most likely continue. Part of Brenda's project was to see if humans could move into the next level of consciousness with the physical form intact and what would be required to make that possible. It was determined pretty quickly that the human form would need to be brought to its highest elevation.

As we progress consciously, we are collecting, integrating, and merging aspects of ourselves to become more fully human. This means we are moving toward a zero-point field where polarity does not exist. The body was designed to be able to dispense information without emotion. As human beings, our emotions, on a cellular level, interrupt the way the body communicates with itself. This causes confusion in the brain as it does not know how to process what it has been presented with. As we clear emotional energy from the cells of our bodies, we allow different aspects and parts of our whole selves to come in and support us more efficiently.

Current times require our cosmic presence as well as our physical body to be on the ground. I agree with what Brenda told me: "Advanced cosmic aspects of our consciousness have to be able to talk to people in a way that they understand." My friend, Vickie B. Majors, created the art for the cover of *Shifting into Purer Consciousness,* the book that I wrote about the ascension process. The artwork is based upon the vision I saw and the experience I had during the writing of that book. August 1, 2011 began a 12-day visitation from an eighth or ninth dimensional aspect (future self) of my soul, which was eventually integrated with my physical body. In the vision that Dr. Caron Goode saw of me during this visitation, my feet were on the Earth in order to function in this dimension, but at the same time, the higher aspect was connected to cosmic knowledge that I can access as needed. This new octave or frequency registering in my body opened or reactivated spiritual gifts that had been dormant for over a decade.

Universal life systems outside of our galaxy are coming together because they realize that what takes place on Earth, in some way, affects every star system. When the merging of soul aspects started for Brenda, her body took a hit. She now realizes that communication with higher aspects of our soul is important in this collaborative process. When she is experiencing something unpleasant in her physical body, she knows it is because of a breakdown in communication. When the body is bypassing normal communication channels and emotions are getting stuck in the limbic system, we can call upon our cosmic technicians to stabilize our bodies. This allows us to walk around comfortably on Earth and bring higher concepts, tools, and expressions into the physical body. This helps the mainstream population to more sanely move through this extreme influx of vibrational acceleration. It allows these frequencies to be translated efficiently in human terms and still hold the vibration of cosmic consciousness.

Through walk-ins, spiritual downloads, and collaboration with galactic beings, the human body is being aligned with the original blueprint for multidimensional awareness. This template is encoded in the matrix (quantum field) because it is already within our DNA. Certain experiences trigger the encoding and we start to feel this as changes within our bodies. We know something is different, and we may have new abilities that prove something is going on. Talking about our experiences causes our fields to connect and allows psychic communication through our sensory faculties.

Lisa Smith

Walk-ins seem to naturally find one another. Lisa Smith had no idea she was a walk-in when she began searching for answers to explain what had happened to her. When she came upon my website, she felt a strong resonance with what she read about walk-ins, yet she thought, "No, this cannot be!" Even though she did not quite understand why, she decided to contact me. I am glad she did because she is a recent walk-in with a very typical story of how things shift after a walk-in occurs.

In March 2012, she was scheduled to do an equinox ceremony. She was normally in her head, and had these kinds of events planned out in detail, but this day she felt as if she was being cocooned—like something had wrapped itself around her, and she was outside of her body. She was flowing from her heart, and felt like she was not herself.

Soon after, Lisa went to a Reiki circle where she received a channeled message from her spirit guides. She learned that she'd had several checkout points in her life in which she could have died, and that there was another pivotal point coming in forty days. If she chose to stay at this time she would have two paths: to continue in her struggle as she had done for the majority of her life, or exit the struggle. She expected a near-death experience or at least some miracle that would help her flow more easily through life. Let me say here that just because you have a pre-incarnation agreement for a soul exchange, does not mean you must go through with it. There is always choice and free will, and a walk-out candidate can say no.

In July, exactly forty days later, Lisa downloaded a Kindle book and was reading it when she felt something "snap" inside. It felt like her soul had been splintered or fractured. She started laughing hysterically thinking this was all a joke. After that, she experienced a lack of memory and started noticing missing spaces of time as she was blogging. There were things she had written that she did not recognize or resonate with. None of the things she had been doing up until that point mattered anymore. But rather than letting up, her life struggle intensified and she wondered if she had chosen the wrong road.

Everything she believed suddenly seemed irrelevant and she no longer knew how to relate to people. She pulled away from the metaphysical community where she had been active, and cancelled the workshops she had written on her itinerary. Part of her wanted to teach the old material, but part of her did not resonate with it and she felt she no longer had a story or identified with her own life. When she did the Reiki attunements, which she had done for years, it felt like an out-of-body experience. It was as if the cellular memory of her body was performing by rote, but the words she was speaking felt like they were coming from somewhere, or someone, else. So, she stopped doing Reiki, which meant she also lost her income. A friend asked her if she thought she might have a mental illness. Lisa felt so strange that she honestly could not answer that question. Yet, in her heart of hearts she knew there was nothing wrong with her and that everything would work out fine. I had the same feelings when my walk-in occurred. I have learned since then that "normal" is just a setting on the clothes dryer and is highly overrated. No one can determine for another person what is right, wrong, or normal for them.

Things really began to unravel for Lisa. She and her husband separated, her mom got sick, and life in general started falling apart. Friends did not understand why she was doing nothing to change her situation. She was going through the motions but not making an effort to control anything. She and her daughter almost ended up homeless before they found a smaller place to live. One person said to her, "You cannot expect Spirit to just waltz in and solve all your problems. You have to take action!" Lisa could not explain what was happening to her, but she did not feel as if she needed to do anything or go back to the metaphysical community. She had an inner calmness and Spirit seemed to be saying to her, "Be still and watch." She felt led to return to school to get her master's degree. She started compiling the material she had written in her journal, trying to remember and put together the missing pieces of the puzzle of her life.

Lisa was about to enter into a two-year shaman program at the end of July 2012 when she decided not to go through with it. Instead, she decided to review the tools and gifts she had already acquired, and re-use them in a new way.

She got a friend request on Facebook from a couple who mentioned a book called *The Joining* by Vishara Veda. The author told about her walk-in experience, and when Lisa read it, she said, "That is what happened to me." The next thing she knew, she was on WE International's blog, where she found me.

Most walk-ins are not a quick in-and-out event in which one person suddenly becomes a different person. It is typical to have a "blending" or transition period in which the two souls try on their new roles, switching back and forth for months, or even years. The natal soul may reside in the auric field of the body and give input and direction about the life in progress. The incoming soul may feel this guidance as something "outside" the body and may ignore those suggestions and decide to do things differently since it is temporarily in charge. Thus, there can be internal conflict as both souls try to "steer the boat." Then, the time is right for the final transfer to occur. This is when we have a "moment" in which something so unusual happens that we never forget it. It is common for a walk-in to look back in retrospect and put two and two together to make three. No, my math is not off; it is just that we never have all the answers and always feel that there is more we could know about this abstract phenomenon.

In our interview, Lisa brought up an interesting point about her past trauma. After her walk-in, the abuse she had experienced as a child was no longer an issue. There was no trigger, anger, emotional response, or relationship to the energy associated with those events. It felt as if those things had never happened, or that they happened to someone else. It took me a decade to arrive at that point in my journey. Lisa, a more recent walk-in, cleared this within months after her exchange.

Lisa says she feels like a totally different person than she was nine months ago and does not know what her next step will be. She is not trying to force anything to happen. She is an observer, and not dictating how her life should be. Now when Lisa does readings for people, she plugs into a higher consciousness to glean information much differently than she did before. Before this shift, she was writing a book. People keep asking her how that and other projects are coming along, but she is not sure she will finish it because her story is still changing. I can so relate to this. The books I wrote prior to this one may not be congruent with the teachings in this book or any future ones I write. I never want to be so set in my ways that I cannot change my beliefs and methods of ministering to others when I find something that works better. But, my previous books and teachings still serve a purpose. There is always going to be someone who is now where I was when I wrote the material. It served me then and it will serve others who are finding the well I have left in the valleys of my own journey.

Like Lisa, I had lofty goals of ascending and transforming my physical body into a light body that could travel to other dimensions. I now realize that we cannot ascend a body or shift its DNA if we are not *in* it! It is super important to integrate and embody higher frequencies and future selves in order to gradually shift and restructure the body. After her walk-in, Lisa began to really value the experience of being a spirit in a human body and she has no plans for checking out. In fact, now that she is fully aware and appreciative of her physical body, she no longer feels like a misfit, as she had for most of her life. But she admits it was challenging at first to stay in her body. She had to touch physical objects whenever she felt like floating away.

About a month after Lisa and I spoke, she reported that she had spent much time in reflection about the process that seems so fluid. She says, "I am learning to appreciate the new experiences I am having, and I am super excited to do the clearing and embark on my new journey. It really is not about figuring out what happened, but rather to embrace who I am at this moment."

That is wisdom we can all embrace!

Diana Morningstar

Diana Morningstar stuttered from the time she was four years old, but she was fluent in the language of the land. This bright, mystical child raised in a large family of Scotch-Irish ancestry had a huge amount of sensitivity toward nature, and would spend hours at the bluff at her grandmother's house, lying in the bluebells and listening to the sounds of the creek. She always felt at one with the earth. "Red," her 6'4" tall high-tempered redheaded grandfather, was intensely weighted by the responsibilities of feeding a large family from the land. Diana's mother was the oldest of his daughters, and her father was also a very intense, driven and fiery man. Her part-Cherokee paternal grandmother, "Granny," was a big woman about six feet tall with broad shoulders, who provided a haven for Diana. She could use an ax and plow the ground alongside any man. Diana has a picture of her holding a fifty-pound fish she had caught. Granny never wrote down much except in the front of her Bible where she recorded the births and deaths of her children; three of them died before they were five years old due to the difficult circumstances. Although she was a powerful woman, she was also very quiet and loving, taking Diana into her brown speckled arms, and holding her in silence while looking into her eyes. Diana experienced her grandmother as the embodiment of unconditional love in her life, and the seed of Grandmother-God took deep root in her prayer life.

When her grandmother died, Diana was about thirty years old, with two small children, and she felt totally lost. She started drinking whiskey when she came home from working long hours in her family's home building business. Seeking something to fill the void, she attended a female minister's journaling workshop in 1988. She began pouring her heart into writing and found that God was speaking to her through the words on the page. Things she didn't want to know or see started being revealed. She began attending a twelve-step Emotions Anonymous group because she was so anxious and depressed. She asked the question we all ask: "Who am I?"

One night, after an abusive family member came home from treatment with a whole new lease on life, she wrote an essay called "The Awakening" that had such a dramatic effect upon her that soon after she was able to speak without stuttering. She was reading books about the divine feminine, and was full to the brim with new ideas, inspiration, and hope; but, she had no way to express it all. One day, while riding a lawn mower, she started praying, "God give me a language, give me a language!" She heard the voice of God in one of the clearest moments, ever. The female voice said, "Sister, I've given you a language. You're just too afraid to use it."

She went home, picked up a book about sacred dance by Carla DeSolo and read on the cover about the lost language of dance, gesture, and movement in communities of faith. A minister invited Diana to start dancing the morning prayers at Scarritt Bennett Conference Center; and, soon she was dancing in churches all over Middle Tennessee and North Alabama. Through dance, she found the expression of everything she couldn't verbalize, and she would lose herself in the dance by going into trance. One time, she was at the First United Methodist Church in Pulaski, Tennessee, in front of 300 mostly conservative ministers—only nine of whom were women. As the pipe organ rang out a hymn, she stood there in front of the golden organ pipes, thinking, "What am I doing in front of all these people? I'm going to dance in church!" She began interpreting, through her dance movements, the song lyrics, "Je-su, Je-su, fill us with your love. Show us how to serve the neighbors we have from you" when a part of her emerged from the trance and she lost all fear and self-consciousness. It was like some part of her disappeared and another spirit came into her body. This walk-in was like the spirit of life, the living water that the scriptures talk about and she realized that the kingdom of heaven is within us and that we are the jewel or pearl of great price. She opened her heart to God, felt spirit come into her bones, her flesh, like never before, and when she finished, some people were in tears. She sat down, took a deep breath, and came back into wakeful reality.

After that, she was invited to dance all over the southeast, doing workshops on "Embodying the Word" and was invited to participate on the National Board of Church Women United, where she served on the diverse Celebrations Committee for four years and planned creative worship services for 1,500 communities across the country. She was the US delegate to World Day of Prayer, which united women from 170 countries in Melbourne, Australia in the name of hope, healing and justice. She preached her first sermon in her home church during this time and began practicing liberation theology, retaining the truth, freedom, peace, and transformation and releasing the oppressive parts of scripture and tradition. She learned how to be kind and gentle with people who were on various spiritual journeys because she had become kind and gentle with herself on her own path. From there, she began reimagining Jesus, reimagining God, reimagining the church, dancing, and doing transformational, grassroots, community organizing in groups where they addressed issues that really mattered. She explored new forms of relationships and the role that sexuality plays in spiritual breakthroughs. Awakening to love and to the spirit of dance, she learned to truly love the world and found herself falling in love with people who also loved the world in this full and fearless way.

Something around the time of that soul exchange pushed her out of the box of trying to confine all her love with one partner. Monogamous relationships with one man no longer worked for her. Her heart would break open for people who came together for social change, playing, developing, and healing themselves in a circle of nurturing love. She left her marriage, ready to love in an open manner. She chose a path of both giving and receiving in this abundantly flowing way and not worrying so much about conforming to cultural norms. Today, at age 57, as a nature-based poet, healer, and community artist she lives at the boundary, choosing a wise, but unconventional path to stay closely in tune with the work and play of her soul. The nature of the flower is to bloom, and like those bluebells that spoke to her on her Grandmother's farm so long ago, she is blooming wherever she is planted.

Casey's Story

Casey's walk-in took place while the previous soul (Jean) was having a test performed.

In February 2009, her body started experiencing massive dizzy spells that caused her vitals to drop, and she would pass out. The episodes got progressively worse and the doctors were stumped. In March of that year, her doctor requested a tilt table test, which measures vital signs in different positions. During the test, her heart rate dropped to a mere thirty beats per minute, and shortly after, she flat lined for about a minute. That was the point when the soul named Casey entered and was braided with Jean for about two and half years. Jean was pretty much in the driver's seat while Casey observed. At the beginning of 2011, the two souls slowly started to trade positions.

In October of 2011, the body fractured her ankle and tore a ligament. Casey later found out that the feet are the holder of our grounding cords. This injury made sense because it partially "broke" Jean's connection with the body. This was the beginning of her exit from Earth life.

Casey started to slowly "awaken" during the fall of 2011; and, by January 2012, she was flying solo as the soul in charge of this incarnation's expression. However, it seemed like her body was rejecting her new soul. Mysterious bruises appeared on her body; she couldn't sleep, had massive headaches, and felt like she wanted to crawl out of her own skin. A friend suggested that she "talk" with her body to explain things and help her calm down.

An ovarian cyst ruptured and left the body very ill and hospitalized in August 2012. While she was in the hospital, Casey was visited by her father, who transitioned to the afterlife about twelve years ago. He informed her that this event was extremely significant because it was her body's way of accepting the new soul and releasing a lot of the repressed anger, emotional pain, and trauma it had held. Since she is a newbie walk-in, her body may still react when something comes up that triggers a cellular memory, but she is able to reassure her body that she is safe and that Casey is not going to leave her.

People have commented on how different "Jean" is, but they think she had an early mid-life crisis and simply turned her life around.

Because we are all unique, your personal story may vary from the ones shared in this book. However, I think you will find enough similarities to help you recognize what might have caused your shift. If you do not see any correlation between these walk-in stories and your own, do not worry. With or without a label for your experience, you can begin to express your soul's authentic purpose right now.

Chapter 7 ~ Moving Forward as a Walk-in

As the Earth's magnetic pull is changing, there continues to be an influx of walk-ins who are trying to integrate higher-vibrating energy into their bodies. Yet, we still have walk-ins from decades ago who have not cleared the negative commitments and energetic imprints of the natal soul and moved into their own mission.

The energy of the previous soul resides in the cellular memory of the body. This energy can be difficult to clear or let go because it feels like our own stuff—and some of it may actually be beneficial for survival. However, some old patterns can limit one from experiencing authenticity, intimacy, and the fulfillment of a spiritual mission as a walk-in soul.

One reason a walk-in might get stuck and not move forward is because they do not realize that much of the negativity they deal with is not their own stuff. Instead, it is the thoughts, emotions, and social programming that have been implanted into the subconscious mind. (I wrote about how to tell when you are carrying someone else's energy in *Whose Stuff Is This? ~ Finding Freedom from the Thoughts, Feelings, and Energy of Those Around You.*) In the case of a walk-in, this "karmic imprint" belongs to the natal soul but it is the responsibility of the walk-in to resolve it.

The human body was not designed to run emotions through its cells. Yet, this is exactly what we have been doing as a species for centuries, and it is killing us. Most of the illnesses and diseases we carry are not ours. We have taken them on by not consciously managing and wisely directing our own energy. When we are submerged in this kind of disharmony, it is hard to get out because we are carrying everybody else's energy. Thus, we become confused with brain fog, headaches, and other symptoms.

It may take some time to integrate the high-vibrational energy of the walk-in soul with the body. The intense energy that comes in with an advanced soul can damage the nervous system of the body—especially if there was a severe trauma or illness prior to the walk-in event. Panic and anxiety attacks, depression, fibromyalgia, chronic fatigue, and other such ailments are common during the integration process. The most important thing a walk-in can do, in the aftermath of a soul exchange, is to nurture and care for the physical body. Speak gently to the inner child that may be freaking out over having a new "parent" in charge. Lots of TLC is required, especially during the first year of integration. Epsom salt baths, healing foods, proper hydration, extra rest/sleep, walks in nature, soothing music, yoga or some form of exercise that gently moves energy while connecting mind, body, and spirit are wonderful tools for helping to calm and heal the body. A holistic practitioner or naturopath may recommend supplements or other treatments to help you get through the adjustment period.

Clearing Energy Imprints

One of the biggest hurdles to overcome, after a walk-in event, is the process of clearing the old energy imprints from the cellular memory of the body. This is a process everyone on the planet must undergo, but walk-ins have a unique desire to "get it done" faster because we are here to cut a path and demonstrate a model that others can follow.

Some people resist this process, which only serves to make it more difficult than it needs to be. We live in the age of grace, which makes it much quicker and easier to move forward in our spiritual evolution. It is like pushing the "easy button" compared to the old ways that advocated "re-living" the emotional trauma of our past. One way we resist the clearing stage is by over analyzing and processing past energy over and over again. Many people are still trying to create the future with the energy of the past. The brain does not know the difference between what is happening now and what happened twenty years ago. So, if you want to experience the pain and victimhood of something that happened way back when you were a teenager, you can do that. Not that I recommend it!

It is great to recognize what is being released, and then consciously chose to let it go, but it is another thing entirely when we allow ourselves to re-run emotional energy through the cells of our body. The idea is to get the stuck emotional energy *out* of the body—not recirculate it—and clear the limbic system of the brain. Do not allow yourself to get stuck when dissolving imprints and releasing patterns that no longer serve you. Brenda Williams once told me that if I cried for more than five minutes over a past issue, I had cried too long. To distract myself from wallowing in this kind of self-pity, I use the Reset Breath© and visualize breathing light into all the cells of the body.

Typically, resistance occurs when we think there is something wrong with our body instead of listening to, and trusting, the messages it is trying to give us. For example, after the eclipse in November 2012, I began to have a sudden Kundalini awakening. For example after the eclipse, in November 2012, I began to have a sudden Kundalini awakening. At that time, I was in the process of writing this book, had just accepted the position as the new president of WE International, and I was contemplating putting together a conference for walk-ins. All of these represented big changes in the way I presented myself to the public. During this time, I was sexually activated and revved up, which also served a purpose; I learned how to direct my life force energy in creative ways to support my life mission (see "Rising Kundalini" in Chapter 3). As the energy arose from my root chakra near the tailbone, I could feel it in all my chakras except for the sixth (forehead) and seventh (crown). The energy was intense in my fifth chakra—the center for self-expression. This created an annoying pressure in my throat and neck, and it felt as if someone had placed their finger on my Adam's apple and left it there. The sensation would come and go randomly throughout the day. It would decrease if I laid down or meditated. It would increase if I got stressed.

Thinking I had too much of a good thing, I stopped taking both of the thyroid supplements that my naturopath had prescribed to me eight months earlier. However, stopping the supplements did not help the situation. A month later, in January, I consulted with him in person, and he recommended getting an ultrasound to see what was manifesting physically. I wanted peace of mind, but I knew that if the ultrasound showed inflammation or cysts, my emotions would cause my lower self to worry and make things worse. I did agree to a thyroid function test, which came back perfectly normal. That was the peace of mind I needed to continue to trust my body and the clearing process it was going through.

One month later, the pressure in my neck had increased and become painful; so, I called on a few friends to pray for me and check in energetically and see what was going on. Dr. Caron Goode recommended nascent iodine to support my thyroid. That was one of the supplements I had stopped taking two months earlier. Since I had some on hand, I took a dose and the pain reduced noticeably within an hour (I am very sensitive to supplements and medications). I felt that the energetic component to this chakra issue was related to returning to public ministry after almost twelve years of peaceful solitude. As an empath, I felt vulnerable regarding this change that would expose me in new ways.

Dr. Tom Goode worked with me energetically over the phone asking the personality (ego) what it was trying to reveal. By being the observer (higher self) and allowing the personality to speak, I learned that it was anger with family, church, and society regarding the way they had taught me to repress my true feelings. This self-expression issue had deep roots— from denying my spiritual/psychic gifts, to telling me how I should *not* explore my own feelings. I acknowledged what was asking to be released and let it go. No tears, no drama. Within hours of working with Tom, and allowing the personality to speak what it needed to say, the pressure decreased until it was barely noticeable, and I felt as though I had turned a corner.

However, two weeks later, the pressure was still there and seemed to be increasing again, so I consented to have an ultrasound of my thyroid. The results were perfectly normal, which told me that there was an energetic component that I still needed to discover. I was beginning to hear things in my mind such as, "*I feel inadequate and not up to the task of taking a leadership role. I do not have the faith needed to move forward in my spiritual mission. I feel stressed out and I do not want to do spiritual work anymore. The Universe is not supporting me in this cause and I'm ready to let it all go. I'm not sure what I believe anymore.*" The real kicker that got my attention was when I heard, "*I'm ready to leave and allow another soul to take this body and carry out this mission.*" I thought my soul was asking for another walk-in and that startled me. I did not realize I was hearing the natal soul's hidden death wish being verbalized from the cellular memory of my soul. After twelve years of clearing karmic imprints of the natal soul, how could there be *anything* left to deal with?

Maxine Taylor is the creator of Star Matrix, her own healing technique that uses the zodiac and spiritual guidance to access information for her clients. She graciously offered to do a healing session with me, and I gratefully accepted. She immediately discovered the problem. I had not cleared the commitments the natal soul had made with my family. Those psychic ties were holding me back, as if a leash were around my neck, from moving forward in my spiritual mission. Our families expect us to be loyal to them. The hidden message is: if you are going to minister or be a leader, you should do it with us, not others. We brought you into the world; we raised you; you *owe* us!

Maxine walked me through the steps of releasing the old commitments made to Mother and accepting my new commitment to Mother. The pressure stopped while I was on the phone with Maxine, and I felt wonderful for the rest of the evening. However, the pressure came back the next day. Back on the phone with Maxine, we completed the Father, Family, and Family Team steps in the clearing and accepting process outlined in her book, *Move into the Magic*. Again, the pressure stopped during the phone call and I felt great. The pressure was back the next day. That's when it dawned on me. Every time I released detrimental energy, higher-vibrating energy would take its place. I would feel better (elated, actually) until more of the old energy came up to be released. It was like trying to put toothpaste back in the tube while squeezing it! This process was not going to stop until all of the emotional and mental energy of the astral body was cleared. I stopped resisting the process, and began thanking my body for it communication effort.

The body and the spirit are meant to operate as a cohesive pair, and any treatment we do to heal any condition works best when both the physical and spiritual components are addressed simultaneously. This disconnect in treatment is where conventional medicine is missing the mark. I noticed a pattern in the tension I was feeling in my neck: it was directly related to any stress I encountered. We know that stress can deplete the body of the vital nutrients and cause cortisol levels to increase, which throws other things in the body, such as hormones, out of balance. I got back on all the supplements my naturopath recommended to support my body while I was clearing the negative commitments and bad messages my natal soul had agreed to.

Some spiritually-evolved friends of mine were also experiencing physical discomfort and strange symptoms during this season. This confirmed to me that we are indeed in a time of rapid ascension and the process is speeding up even more. We were reminded that the physical body needs more rest while the DNA is shifting and we are creating and tuning up our merkabah (light body) for inter-dimensional travel. Naps have become our afternoon ritual.

Everything is energy. Whatever begins and is allowed to grow in the mental or emotional bodies eventually manifests in the physical body. Once I cleared the imprints, the contraction in my throat relaxed and the uneasiness went away. I had heeded the message and there was no need for the discomfort to continue. What would have happened had I not honored and stayed true to my inner knowing that this situation was energetic in nature? If I had continued to focus on the problem rather than discovering the message my body was trying to give me, I would likely have manifested a physical illness that could have been revealed on lab tests. Instead, being gentle with my body and loving myself in spite of what was going on, the neck pressure subsided on it own.

If you are consistently doing some type of spiritual purification to cleanse and clear your Earth personality, you will notice that you are uncovering the truth of your beautiful authentic self. As a result of your practice, your vibration will raise and take you to new levels of awareness. But, these levels tend to create ascension symptoms or have an "initiation" attached to them like the one I just mentioned. The initiation process occurs as changes are being made to our DNA at a subatomic or molecular level, or as emotional energy is being released from the body. About 99 percent of what we are clearing is a result of emotional energy stuck in the limbic system and cells of the body.

When I get into a funky mood as a result of this purification process, my husband says that I am like a machine that is "down for maintenance." There are times when things my ego self says or does some very unbecoming things while its parts are scattered all over the floor! Fortunately, my husband does not take anything too seriously and pays no attention to the woman behind the curtain when she is undergoing intense periods of reprogramming. I am thankful to live with a man who reminds me to leave well enough alone. I will pass his words of wisdom on to you, "Step away from the trash! Stop analyzing and trying to fix the broken parts!" My empathic and walk-in friends want to clone him.

These "setbacks" can be very disturbing if we think that *we are* our thoughts, emotions, or 3-D personality rather than the spirit observer watching ourselves. It can seem like we are taking a step backward in the ascension process when this happens, but actually the opposite is true.

Maintaining Your Personal Eighteen Inches

The next hurdle in maintaining your own personal space is related to the first hurdle and applies to everyone on Earth. Your personal space is an egg-shaped bubble or aura that extends about eighteen inches outside your physical body. (Your aura and soul essence can expand far beyond this range.) This eighteen inches is *all* the energy we are responsible for maintaining and holding steady! We make it difficult on ourselves by trying to maintain more than this, or by trying to alter other people's fields. We do this by sending our thought forms and emotional energy where they do not belong: back to the past (regrets), into the future (worrying), or to someone and the drama they are creating. Being able to hold resonance in your own vibrational field and keep it clear from the energy of those around you is the most helpful thing you can do assure inner peace. It is from this space that you create everything you encounter in your personal world.

We are taught to give and give, and sometimes take a little. But, taking is not the same as receiving. Being able to receive is a big part of the shift in consciousness, not only for us personally as individuals, but also culturally, globally, and cosmically. The truth is that we are not responsible for healing or "fixing" other people. If you see someone who is suffering, you can have compassion for them without getting entangled in their personal drama or the mess you may perceive that they are creating in their lives. I know that that sounds rather harsh and hardnosed. That's because we have been taught to care for other people by taking on their suffering. Martyrdom is considered to be a virtue by many religions, but all it really does is keep people from taking responsibility for their own lives and what they are creating. Parents do this with their kids when they do not allow them to experience the consequences that come from the choices they make.

Let's say that someone comes to you in distress. Perhaps he or she is experiencing illness, dysfunctional relationships, a lack of money, loss of job, unruly rebellious kids, etc. You can try to correct or heal this person's symptoms, but that does not do any good. You have to go to another level in order to help that person embody their soul vibration. When they do that, things shift to a place of synchronicity and harmony.

By the way, it is good when your life is falling apart. It is not a negative thing or an indication that you did something wrong, or that you are a failure, or that you cannot get your act together. There is no need to judge it or think it is your fault or that someone is a victim. This happens because we are out of harmony with everything on a physical level: the cycles of the moon, the Earth's vibrations, our spiritual inner knowing, etc. Humanity is sleepwalking and these life crises offer the opportunity to wake up. It might feel a little painful when you first wake up from the dream and realize that you created all you are now experiencing. However, you get to rebuild it on a higher level and make it much happier.

Overcoming Confusion & Getting "Unstuck"

There is a TV show called *Dog Whisperer* in which Cesar Millan retrains the dog owners whenever their dogs are aggressive or poorly behaved. The dogs are actually reacting to their owners, who have unconscious internal fear and chaos. We humans react similarly when fear and other emotions are stuck in our limbic system. The limbic system is comprised of the thalamus, hypothalamus, cingulate gyrus, amygdala, hippocampus, and basal ganglia. This is the area of the brain that regulates emotion and memory, and directly connects the lower and higher brain functions.

The human form was not created to process emotions in the body. Therefore, when our mind and emotions are not aligned with our higher truth, it can cause physical pain, illness, depression, insomnia, financial difficulties, etc. These are signs that something is out of sync inwardly and that the body is processing emotional energy in its cells. Breathing light into the brain and the Reset Breath© can help clear emotional energy from the limbic system. Breathing light into the brain is a simple visualization in which you use your intention to move light into the brain as you breathe in and then release impurities on the exhale.

The following technique, known as the Reset Breath©, comes from Brenda Williams and her work with the high councils of off-planet genetic technicians. To receive maximum benefit, it is recommended that you use the Reset Breath© frequently during your day. You will know that you have fully integrated this practice when you no longer have to remember to use it.

The Reset Breath©

Normally, this technique is demonstrated in three segments: telling, showing, and doing. This helps to integrate the technique by allowing the senses to hear it, see it, and do/feel it. But since you and I are not sitting together face to face, you cannot hear me speak the directions or watch me demonstrate the breath. The Reset Breath© is easy enough that you can learn to do it by simply reading the directions. However, Brenda does have a video on her website, http://earthproject777.com, if you would like to follow her in the demonstration.

Our normal breathing pattern is an inhale followed by an exhale. The Reset Breath© begins with an exhale in order to signal the brain that something is about to change and we want it to pay attention. Breaking the cycle alerts the brain that a change is being requested and that it needs to integrate the new information that it is receiving.

Begin by counting aloud: one, two, three, four, five. Immediately exhale or blow out through your mouth. Next, inhale through your nose. It is important to bring your breath deep into your diaphragm, keeping your shoulders relaxed as you inhale. Next, exhale fully and completely through your mouth.

As heart rhythms, breathing patterns, and brain waves are synchronized, the physiology begins to shift. You may feel this as peaceful energy flowing in your body.

I have found it helpful to speak a new truth that I wish to integrate. These are usually positive "I AM" statements or affirmations.

A component that works well with the Reset Breath© is a technique known as Quiet Touch©, which was also originated by Brenda Williams. Combined, this technique is known as RBQT©. You might use this anytime you feel yourself in a place of anxiety or fatigue, or when you are in an environment that leaves you feeling uncomfortable or disengaged.

Quiet Touch©

The human body's innate ability to self-regulate, combined with the specific positioning of Quiet Touch©, triggers the internal encoding within the body.

When we place our left palm at the center of the chest, we are connecting two electromagnetic fields. This connection creates a resonance that results in what some refer to as the "still point"—a moment when we are connected in perfect resonance to all that exists. Source to Source.

Begin this exercise by firmly placing the palm of your left hand comfortably on your chest. (Observe that the hand and arm are in a relaxed position).

Notice and observe any sensations that you might experience. Do the Reset Breath© and continue to observe the rhythm of your breathing. Take as much time as you require.

Reposition the left palm at the center of your chest and continue to be present and observe any sensations or thoughts that might arise. This is the time when your intention is to observe and notice—to become the observer of yourself, your physical form, and the environment around you.

Allow yourself to feel the bliss of the energy flowing through your body and aura. Bliss is the effect of oneness. When you move into that place of joy, you feel that you can conquer the world. There is no experience of physical pain, mental stress, or worry. You have clear thoughts, experience emotional freedom, and feel peaceful throughout your body. Even if you only hold this blissful feeling for two seconds, make it your goal each day to get to this place. Being in this place of bliss for just a few minutes will positively affect your whole day. The more you practice this, the easier it will be to get to this place of centeredness. Soon you will be able to hold this feeling throughout your day, even while focused on others tasks.

As an additional experience, switch to the right palm and notice if there is any difference. However, it is important to remember that you place your *left* hand on your chest to receive maximum benefit from Quiet Touch©.

Sensitivity

Nowadays, the integration period is not as devastating, and walk-ins are not alienating from families and friends like they did twenty years ago. Even so, if you think being a walk-in is appealing, think again! The work involved in the aftermath of a soul exchange is anything but glamorous.

The walk-ins and empaths I talk to in my coaching practice are very sensitive, mainly because they have not learned to manage what is going on in their mind, emotions, and aura (the personal space around the body). The physical body is surrounded by an aura and many subtle bodies: etheric, emotional, mental, astral, causal, celestial, and ketheric bodies. The lower four layers store memories, thoughts, beliefs, emotions, karmic patterning, and other data regarding everything that an individual experiences.

A baby has the safety and comfort of its parent's love and protection at birth, and does not have language skills, the ability to move about, or the responsibility to make choices that affect others. This gives the soul time to adjust while the body gains motor skills and collects life experiences and information to help it navigate. When a soul walks into a body that can already walk, talk, drive a car, think logically, and make decisions, it is expected to continue to carry out adult responsibilities such as feeding itself, making a living, caring for children, balancing a checkbook, etc.

Naturally, a walk-in feels strange coming into a complex system already in place that instantly begins making demands of them. They feel a temptation to dissociate or float off to somewhere outside of the body—perhaps to a gentler place that resembles the dimension or reality that they came from. So, the challenge for a new walk-in is to be fully present in the body. Actually, this is a challenge for most humans. Many people self-medicate through a variety of substances and addictions that keep them from facing the chaos they or others have created. You see this being played out in mindless chatter, unconscious eating habits, and lack of attention to the task at hand. I used to think that multitasking was the only way to get a lot done in a short amount of time. I now know that abiding in the quantum field is the best way to create because it allows the universe to support me and do things on my behalf, such as bringing people into my life that are a bigger blessing than I could ever have imagined.

Staying in the Body

It is not uncommon to continue to experience dissociative episodes after having a near-death experience, a walk-in, or an energy download. However, it is very important to stay in the body after such a blast of energy in order to anchor the faster vibrating energy and function as a spirit in a human body. Yet, this is one of the greatest challenges for a new walk-in.

We ignore way too many kinesthetic sensations and this is what puts us on autopilot and disconnects us from our bodies. That, of course, keeps us from using our body as the sensory or guidance tool it was created to be. The way to get fully present in your body is to really notice how the body feels at any given moment. Our body's sensations are one of the many ways our higher guidance speaks to us, but so few listen—some are even afraid of what they might feel. The advice I give my coaching clients is to begin interacting with the five physical senses—engage constantly. These are some things you can do every day at any time to become more aware and get in touch with your body.

- Notice where your body is touching the surface upon which you are sitting or lying. How does it feel?
- Slowly chew your food; really taste it and feel the texture. Lick your fingers!
- Talk aloud to yourself, and listen to the guidance you hear. Ask questions of your guidance—you may find yourself speaking out the answers.
- Look at yourself in the mirror. Do not judge; just observe and be okay with what you see.
- Touch your body and allow sensual feelings to arise.
- Pay attention to how it feels to release waste from your body when you use the toilet.
- Listen to your own voice as you speak.
- Feel the fabric of the clothes you are wearing.
- Smell your skin.
- Notice the temperature of your body. Are you warm, hot, or cold?
- Sit still and listen to what you hear around you.
- Pet an animal, and notice how the fur feels.

These are so simple, but they remind us to pay attention to our feelings. I encourage you to explore more ways to tune into the messages of your body as you practice simple things like the ones listed above.

I know this works. It not only helps you stay in your body and appreciate all its functions, it helps you begin to love yourself unconditionally. Here is an unedited excerpt from an email a client sent me after our first coaching session in which I asked her to try the body sensing exercise.

When my husband came home last night, I told him that I needed some down time and went to bed around 9 p.m., which is early for me. I was very thoughtful about everything I did. For example, when I washed my face, it was amazing to realize that I do not look in the mirror when I wash my face. I did so last night and spent several minutes getting re-acquainted with it and noticed the things that have changed.

I burned some essential oils and did my grounding and centering exercise. I lay in bed for several minutes to simply listen to body. I learned many things:

I noticed that I clench my stomach. I had to remind myself several times to let go and relax those muscles. I suspect that I have spent a good majority of my life with a clenched belly. So I rubbed my stomach and did a lot of deep breathing.

I also heard a little voice that kept telling me that my body was a work of art–a sculpture. That it needed to chip away at the unnecessary parts (extra weight), but I was working against it. "Just stretch" kept looping through my head. So I am considering yoga or Pilates.

I kept going back to two specific events in my life. Both were very negative experiences and each time, I gained a significant amount of weight (30+ pounds). Again, this voice spoke, telling me it is time to forgive, let go, and move on. I found this significant because I hadn't consciously thought about either incident in a very long time. I actually fought these thoughts initially, but I know there is a message there for me. Now that I am not afraid, I am willing to look for clarity.

I woke up this morning very clear headed. I have been fighting a cold/sinus infection for days. Yet, I feel about 60-70 percent better! Although I am not excited about my job, I am not feeling the dread that I wake up with most mornings.

I also appreciate your article on feelings vs. emotions. I can say that my intuition "gut feeling" is almost always right, even when I was a little girl. Yet I have failed or been less successful because I second guessed myself (or allowed others to do it for me).

The more you practice this type of mindfulness, the more you will stay in the now moment and hear your higher guidance. It will also quiet much of the mind chatter that rules our thoughts. With consistent practice, you will gain the ability to make conscious choices about what you feel, say, and do. I would love to know what you discover by doing this simple exercise.

Physical Healing or Adjustment

"Healing may not be so much about getting better, as about letting go of everything that isn't you - all of the expectations, all of the beliefs - and becoming who you are." ~ Rachel Naomi Remen

Unlike our brains and bodies, the soul does not need healing. It is already perfect. The brain has been conditioned to believe in separation rather than oneness, wholeness, and wellness. Suffering is the byproduct of dysfunctional thinking. Because the body follows whatever instructions it is given, either consciously or subconsciously, the brain is also the key to healing the physical and emotional bodies. Therefore, we need to focus on educating or re-patterning the brain, personality, emotions, and ego (small self) to accept higher vibrations. This helps us stop reacting to life and other people's situations through our emotions, which causes us to get enmeshed in their energy and chaos. We are here to learn how to control our emotions, manage our body, and know that we are in charge of our life. If we begin to consciously heal our brain, it moves us toward shifting the body out of disease mode.

When you buy a used vehicle or house, the former owner may have left some mechanical or deferred maintenance that needs to be tended to. The same is true with walk-ins. The natal soul may have left physical, social, or emotional situations for the walk-in soul to resolve.

In addition to wading through the disorientation typically associated with walking in, the physical body must deal with the influx of higher vibrating energy that the walk-in soul emanates. It can feel like a 220-volt current moving through a circuit wired for 110-volt current. This amplification may cause the body's nervous system to feel as though it has been fried. Nervousness, shaking, energy surges, tension, anxiety, panic attacks, headaches, body aches, emotional outbursts, and physical illnesses are possible side-effects you may have while aligning the body with the vibration of the new soul. Keeping the body nourished and cleared of toxins is very important during this phase.

Earth is moving through a unique cosmic alignment in our galaxy and solar/planetary system. In addition to the accelerated energies and cosmic influences this brings to Earth, we also have toxins on the planet that are compromising our health. There is not much we can do to avoid these highly-charged cosmic frequencies and environmental pollution. However, we are in charge of what we put into and onto our bodies. It is a matter of loving ourselves enough to take the extra time and effort to pay attention to what we are eating, drinking, watching, listening to, and exposing our skin and lungs to as well as whom we are associating with.

When a soul comes into the Earth plane through a walk-in situation, it may miraculously restore the vibrational purity of the body. Avoiding toxins and keeping the system clean will help much toward integrating the higher frequencies.

Nervous System and Endocrine System

There are two systems in our bodies that are affected, sometimes in a dramatic way, after a walk-in: the nervous system and the endocrine system. The endocrine system includes the third eye, pineal gland, thyroid, thymus, pancreas, and the organs/systems these govern. You may experience an expansion in your third eye, and suddenly be able to see everyone's auras and life drama, which can be very disconcerting.

The light and energy that moves through the body during a walk-in event may cause the body's nervous or endocrine system to be disrupted. You might experience dips in thyroid function, which means you might need thyroid support. If your thymus or immune system is affected, you could experience a low-grade fever, constant allergies, fatigue, a low level of energy, muscle and joint aches, digestive trouble, or other problems. Please do not ignore what is going on with your body. If you have these symptoms, find a naturopath in your area, and get help. To find a naturopath in your area, see http://goo.gl/ACzMt. Feel free to discuss your journey in WE International's support group at http://Facebook.com/walkinevolution.

The human nervous system has two major components: the Peripheral Nervous System and the Central Nervous System. Within the Peripheral Nervous System is the Autonomic Nervous System that is responsible for several involuntarily functions such as metabolism, heart rate, breathing, and digestion. So, if your nerves are experiencing energy overload, you may not be able to digest the foods that you used to eat. Animal protein or dairy maybe too heavy. Your energy may burn out quickly, and as a result, you end up craving carbs and sugary foods that raise your blood sugar and energy level. However, if you keep eating all of these inflammatory and acidic foods while unable to process them, the yeast overgrowth they create may eventually perforate the intestines and cause leaky gut syndrome. The idea is to eat lightly and stay away from sugars and addictive foods such as alcohol and caffeine that tax the nervous system. Some walk-ins find it helpful to avoid gluten and eat organic and plant-based diets that are easily digested while keeping the body grounded and providing energy.

Your body may need energy work or chiropractic adjustments. Walking, or low-impact exercise such as swimming or yoga, can help to keep energy moving and clear the lymphatic system. Yoga also helps connect the mind and spirit with the body.

Expansion

Not all of our spirit will fit into a human body. In fact, only a very small portion actually resides in the body. Rather, it encompasses our aura and extends indefinitely above our heads. Some parts of our spirit interface or live in other planetary systems and other dimensions. So, when a new aspect of spirit comes to dwell in the body, a feeling of expansion may occur. This newly arrived soul aspect may feel confined and try to stretch the body to accommodate its enormous vibration. Many bodies gain weight soon after a walk-in occurs because of this.

The incoming soul can no longer see from the same vantage point that it did from outside the body and it may try to open the body's third eye or alter its physical vision. It may be thinking, *Turn on the windshield wipers. I cannot see through this foggy window!* or *Turn up the volume. I cannot hear the voice of my guidance!* Thus, the eyes may begin to see shadowy figures or flashes of color, be sensitive to light, or the vision may go in and out of focus like a camera. The ears may ring or buzz, and hearing may be heightened. If the noise is too much, the ears may try to close down the interference and cause the body not to hear as keenly as before.

You may feel a sense of expansion, as if you are in an altered state at times—even when you are not meditating. This is certainly not a bad thing, but staying in the body is important if you want to function in the 3-D world. So, remember to connect with your body's senses and physical feelings whenever you feel spacey.

Relationships

The walk-in soul has its own unique personality and may want to make changes to the body, life, and relationships that the natal soul had in place. Therefore, it is common for him or her to detach and let go of people who were part of the life before the walk-in. As part of establishing their new identity, some walk-ins change jobs or professions. Name changes are also common.

While those close to me sensed that something was different, most of my family still does not know that the soul now in this body is not the one they knew when I was younger. They saw the drastic changes that took place in my life between 1999 and 2001, but most were not ready to accept an explanation about my walk-in, even if I had known what was happening then.

Being a walk-in could explain why your family seemed to reject you, especially when you first came in. You were wearing the same flesh that your biological mother brought into this plane, but you are not the same soul she nurtured. While you appeared in the same body that was used as a vehicle for your children to enter this earth plane, you are not the same soul who raised them.

Walk-ins tend to view relationships differently than most people. Because they operate with a multidimensional view of oneness with God, nature, and others, they may not play the role or fit the mold of traditional relationships. As a walk-in, you may or may not have a soul contract with the person that the natal soul was intimate with. You are still responsible for completing the contract in some way—either by continuing the relationship or by peacefully ending it in a mutually agreeable manner. I walked out of my first marriage within hours of walking into this body. Fortunately, not everyone is compelled to make such a drastic change. You may have to decide whether or not you can live authentically with the "inherited" spouse or partner of the natal soul.

Our society teaches us to be co-dependent rather than inter-dependent. Thus, we look to others to define who we are, fulfill us emotionally, or take care of us physically or financially. In other words, we expect another person to meet all of our needs. Walk-ins who inherit a lot of emotional baggage come into relationships dragging along past hurts and wounds, feelings of inadequacy and inferiority, and other limiting beliefs. When one partner expects the other partner to tend to his or her neediness, the relationship is doomed from the start. One person usually ends up being a martyr or feeling possessed by the other. Both partners are unfulfilled. This type of relationship is counterproductive to a walk-in who came to serve humanity with a higher purpose.

We have to detach from the mindset of our culture, religion, politics, military, government, and money system in order to come into our own center and find ourselves, our personal energy, and our life-force. We are in the world, but not of it.

Meditation

One way to get to your divine center is through meditation. Combined with RBQT©, you should experience joy during meditation because it puts you into a place of oneness—the still point. If we hold a state of oneness in our mind and body, we radiate this transmission, and people automatically resonate to that frequency when they are near us. When we are able to embody oneness and we lay our hands on people, something happens.

Sometimes when people meditate, they go into other dimensions and get frightened. Some may have visitations of light beings or family/friends on the other side making contact. There is no need to be afraid of these experiences. They are simply conveying a message that we are not alone and that they are supporting us. Religion has taught us to fear what we do not understand. If your mind starts making up a fearful story, disengage from it and do not give it any power.

Finding Your Mission

Many people say they do not know what it is that they are here to do. The answer is really quite simple. If there is something that you desire or know you would be good at, it is likely your life's path. You can probably name that desire right now. Whatever brings you joy is your soul's intended path.

So, what is it that keeps you from making that a reality? Fear that you will fail? Fear that you cannot make enough money to support yourself in that field? Fear of . . . what? These are the things that you must clear in order to find your purpose in life. So, stop doing what makes you miserable and start doing what brings you joy. You will be supported as you follow your bliss.

There is a statement of intent in my book, *Shifting into Purer Consciousness*, that will help you create affirmations that will help to reprogram your mind to believe that you can do whatever you have been sent here to do. The Universe would not send a highly-evolved soul to this planet without making provisions for its success. The limitation is only in your mind.

Once you move past the fear and beliefs that keep you from stepping out in faith, you will soon notice your mission beginning to unfold effortlessly as things naturally fall into place. It is a process of letting go of the scarcity mindset of the small self and embracing an empowered, unlimited view of yourself as a divine being.

One of the easiest ways to overcome fear is to experience the intense and beautiful loving presence of your God-self (monad). The feelings that wash over your body, mind, and emotions can create a union with Spirit like no other you have ever experienced. Meditation times will become sweeter as you feel drawn into the Sacred Heart, even on a moment's notice or in the midst of chaos. Tapping into this state of bliss, which RBQT© can help facilitate, will cause things to shift effortlessly.

In the physical realm, begin to take baby steps in the direction of your dreams. For example, if you enjoy singing and see yourself making a living by using your vocal talent, sing every chance you get. Sing in the shower, sing the car, sing while in meditation, etc., but also volunteer your talent as a gift to the world perhaps by singing in your meditation group, at a nursing home, or other public venue. Get into a community choir, form a band, and seek gigs where you can share your talent. Every step you take toward manifesting your dream moves you closer to being able to earn an income from what you do.

This is exactly how I built my business, Writers in the Sky Creative Writing Services (http://writersinthesky.com). I started in 2003 by following my guidance to write a book and not worry about what to do with the final product. By the time I finished writing that book, I had been led to share what I had learned about self-publishing. Then, I sensed it was time to offer my writing services to others; so, I researched how to start a small business, and created a website. Each time I took action on what I heard, I received guidance for the next step to take. With each client project, I learned more about writing, editing, marketing, business management, and customer relations. Soon, I had more business than I could handle on my own, and I formed an alliance of writers and editors to take some of the projects.

You can use affirmations as a reminder to keep your focus on what you want to create rather than what you are experiencing from a past creation. Affirmations are especially helpful when life situations seem to be going in a counterproductive direction. I relied upon them every day while building my writing business and spiritual ministry. I was tempted to give up my dream and go back to a corporate job at least once a week, but I persevered. The business is still flourishing ten years later.

You can conquer large tasks by just doing what you feel led to do at any particular moment. Simply ask for your next step every day and act on the guidance you receive. After one year, you will have taken 365 steps, and will be able to see the progress you have made.

The Difference between Feelings and Emotions

It is very important to be able to distinguish the difference between emotions and feelings. Very simply put, emotions carry energetic signatures of the past, and are based on thoughts. Feelings are recognized through the physical body, and tell you what is going on for you in the present moment.

Feelings and emotions can both have an effect upon your body and mind. Because they are rooted in some past experience, emotions try to rule your choices by reminding you of consequences, and keeping you stuck in your past. Generated by the small self, they are usually triggered by a current dilemma that reminds you of what happened in a similar previous experience. Because they tend to be fear-based and can contain other people's energy, emotions are very unreliable and self-limiting.

Feelings are a result of the life force energy flowing through you as they register a response within your physical body. Unlike emotions, feelings are yours and yours alone. They are painstakingly honest as they urge you to take a look at what is transpiring for you in the here and now. They are not based on past regrets/experiences, nor are they concerned about the future. Therefore, they may encourage you to give up an old belief pattern or shift into a new way of living or viewing life. Feelings give you options and allow you to be in control of what action to take based upon the energetic information they provide.

Emotions are not real—they can and will lie to you. Feelings are real, and always tell you the truth, even though you may not like their message or wish it were different.

The Feelings Test

In Chapter 8 of my book, *Whose Stuff is This?* I shared the following exercise that I believe will help you determine whether you are experiencing an emotion or a feeling. It will also help you make decisions based upon how the vibration or energy of that decision feels in your body. Walk-in souls have a lot of these kinds of decisions to make—especially when they are new to the body. This is a great exercise to help the soul become aware of the body, and stay fully present in it.

Begin by thinking about a situation you are currently in. Perhaps you are considering a new business venture, a change in residence, leaving or beginning a relationship, or maybe you sense that a potential walk-in soul is requesting an exchange. You have at least two choices to make: either go for the opportunity or turn it away—at least for the time being.

Take a deep breath to center your thoughts, and find the still place (sacred heart) within. Become aware of how your body feels in this neutral, natural state. Put aside any worry about what will happen in the future, and honestly acknowledge whatever you feel right now. This does not mean you will act upon it—just feel it.

1. As you release the breath, hold the thought that you will accept the opportunity being presented to you.
2. Now come back to a neutral point, and think of the situation again. This time consider turning away the opportunity. Did you feel any kind of shift in your body or the field around you?

Which consideration made you feel peaceful, happy, or relaxed?

Which consideration made you feel tense, uneasy, or agitated?

Did you hold your breath when considering either thought?

The thought that made you feel relaxed or at ease is your true desire, and more than likely the choice you should make.

Sometimes you may get an equal feeling for either option. For example, my husband was "invited" to attend a meeting at work. It was not mandatory, and he really did not want to go, but there were certain expectations that he be there. He did the above exercise and noticed that one choice did not generate any more feeling than the other. In cases like this, I suggest that you consider yourself first—I know that is not easy for those who come from a religious upbringing, co-dependent society, or dysfunctional family. Decide which choice brings you the most joy or the least amount of personal stress or inconvenience. If my husband were to attend that meeting, it would put him in afternoon traffic, and take him more than an hour to drive twelve miles home. This would cause him to rearrange or cancel his plans to go to the gym for some much-needed exercise. If your decision does not have a personal stress factor involved, if it does not infringe upon your well-being, and if others would benefit by your participation, go for it. Just make sure that your choices are always aligned with your true feelings/inner guidance and not by your emotions or someone's neediness or manipulation.

Chapter 8 ~ Facilitating a Soul Exchange

Let me begin this chapter by stating that a walk-in/out does not occur simply because you wish to leave your body or escape the Earth life you have created by the choices you have made. In other words, you cannot choose to have an advanced soul take over the reins because you are unhappy with your life or entertaining suicidal thoughts. Soul exchanges are pre-incarnation contracts and are negotiated on a higher level without the input of the ego. When your ego offers your body up to another soul and there is no pre-arranged plan in place, you risk having a lower-vibrating entity take possession of your physical body or attach to your auric field. Chances are, there is already an entity at work causing you to feel this hopeless. I suggest you work with an energy healer to help you get free of this detrimental energy. Then, you will be able to think clearly enough to make decisions about how to "un-create" the things that have gone wrong in your life, and begin to create what you do want.

We have do free will, and our higher self can veto a walk-out/in when an opportunity is presented to us. Before my soul exchange took place in 1999, I had two near-death experiences in which there was negotiation in higher realms to determine if the time was right for the soul swap. Prior to being taken to an emergency surgery in 1988, my natal soul felt certain that she was leaving the planet, but the time was not right. She was very angry and disappointed to still be in body when she awoke in the recovery room.

The smaller self or personality (ego) is not the one who ultimately decides when a soul will come into the body and when one will leave. The ego often creates death urges that create exit points, but even during those "opportunities" the perfected soul (higher self), soul group members, and monad decide the best course of action. That's why not every near-death experience or suicide attempt results in a soul swap.

Having said all that, I realize there are times when someone just "knows" that a walk-in is about to occur for them. Perhaps this person is a revolving door walk-in and has had several soul swaps or walk-along experiences. If you strongly feel that you are destined for a soul exchange, you will likely begin to have internal signs—dreams, spontaneous visions, apparitions/visitation by angels—that lets you know you have "permission" and are being guided toward this experience. You may be aware of another soul or higher dimensional being in your field who is willing to wear your body and resolve any existing emotional patterns. These are the ones this chapter was written for.

There are people, whose mission is to help walk-out souls find their way home. Some people are able to facilitate cord exchanges for souls who are ready to pass the baton. One day, you may be called upon to help facilitate one of these exchanges or simply hold space as someone has this experience. The following tips may be helpful.

What to Do Before a Soul Exchange

When a soul's work or Earth contract is complete, it may be offered the opportunity of a soul exchange. Even if the natal soul's work is not complete, the incoming soul may be allowed to come in if it agrees to complete any unresolved issues for the soul it is replacing. Again, this decision is determined by higher guidance and according to Divine Plan.

Soul exchanges are much like a hospice transition or a physical death. Here are some tips on how to prepare when someone is about to experience a conscious soul exchange.

- Most conscious walk-outs communicate with the walk-in soul for weeks or months prior to the actual swap date. The walk-out soul should make sure that the walk-in soul is of the light and is not going to harm the body or anyone else. The best way is to simply ask internal questions and use the "The Feelings Test" in chapter 7 to notice vibrational shifts in your body when considering the decision.
- Allow the outgoing soul to enjoy a favorite food, visit a favorite place, or do whatever brings a sense of closure or completion before departing.
- Nourish the body well to make the vessel as clean and healthy as possible.
- If the departing soul is troubled, overly tired, or in any way emotionally charged, it is highly recommended to retrieve soul parts.
- Clean and clear past karma of the departing soul to help "get the house in order." The departing soul may need to be forgiven or offer forgiveness to another person. They may ask that this be done on their behalf if they feel unable to do so before leaving.
- The departing soul should disclose whatever needs to be taken care of and know that someone will complete any unfinished business in his/her absence.
- Set the "nest" with clear and high-frequency energies like you might for a physical birthing: a quiet, peaceful, and loving environment without intrusions so the body can simply lay down and go through the cord exchange.

- The soul needs to know that it is loved. Give thanks for the work it accomplished while in body.
- The soul needs to know when it has left the body. Anyone attending the death may gently place a hand on the arm of the body so it can feel... and then not feel ... and know they are outside of/released from the physical body.

What to Do After a Soul Exchange

Many times walk-ins have a difficulty adjusting to Earth life because it seems so backwards and primitive. I have coached many a client who is a walk-in and has decided they do not want to be here or feel like the walk-in was a mistake. It is important to help the soul integrate with the body and accept responsibility for whatever situation it is dealing with. This is best done by offering love and kindness to the body and the inner child that may be exhibiting a lot of fear over what is transpiring.

After the exchange has occurred, it is important to continue to maintain a safe place for the soul to experience the energy of higher dimensions. Often a greater realization is given to the soul because it is still in the presence of multidimensional beings in a higher field as it acclimates. In the earlier stages, a walk-in may have recognition of other-worldly beings or nature spirits such as elementals, depending upon the resonation of the incoming soul during that phase of integration. All seems to become unified as integration continues.

It is common for the body's need for rest to change after a walk-in. Some nights will be highly activated with so much light and energy that you may be unable to sleep. Other times, you may sleep for twelve to fourteen hours straight. The need for extra sleep may last for days, weeks, or several months so give your body the time it needs to fully adjust.

Eat to "fuel the situation" and forget whatever the latest diet or eating trend might be. Listen to your own body.

Getting together with other walk-ins and/or highly-evolving beings can be beneficial to help hold the field of energy steady. The new soul may go through the "Am I going crazy?" or "What is happening to me?" stage and need to share what is occurring. That is the main reason I organize events that allow starseeds, lightworkers, walk-ins, and healers to connect. You will find these workshops listed on my website: WeAre1InSpirit.com.

Continue cleansing the vehicle (physical body) and raising the vibration by using products that support the higher electrical current. These include living or raw foods, organic fruits and vegetables, non-fluoridated water, unrefined, non-GMO, and non-chemically treated foods, etc. Breathing techniques, yoga, stretching, meditations, and adequate rest are also useful to help the body shift and match frequencies along the way.

Much like shifting gears on a car, coming to a neutral point is very much a part of the integration process. The soul needs permission to do nothing more than follow the guidance as it comes in. We do not have to know everything that is transpiring; we do not have to be in control; there is no need to focus on the work of the new soul until everything is integrated and functioning. Sometimes a soul wants to hit the ground running toward its mission. Until the integration process is complete, it is best to simply focus on stabilizing and caring for the body that may have gone through some trauma prior to or as a result of the walk-in. Before making any big decisions, assess what the body and emotions are ready to handle, and then determine the appropriate way to proceed. We do not have to know or control everything that is transpiring. Keep life simple and acquire only what is truly necessary in each moment.

Let nature support you in the integration process. It was very warm that September day as a friend and I were sitting at a picnic table in a park. As my friend was demonstrating how to be "one with nature" the cicadas, that were all around us, seemed to respond to what she was doing. When I put my thumb and first finger together and spoke, "I intend harmony in this space now," the cicadas' humming noise increased by at least 100 percent and the wind kicked up, causing leaves to shimmer and dance in the treetops. I thought it was just a coincidence at first, so I tried it again (and again and again) just to see if it could be reproduced. As I went about exploring my surroundings, the cicadas would calm back down to a low buzz. If I spoke to the nature beings, I was amazed at how they responded to my intention.

Chapter 9 ~ Finding Community

In my interaction with other walk-ins, most mention a profound change they experienced and can reference an event or period of time in their lives when they began to feel different. Yet, many cannot explain it to themselves, much less try to relate the experience to others. Most do not have friends with whom they can share this strange event. Therefore, there is a need to establish a connection with like-minded people who can support those who are on walk-in assignments. Thankfully, this is easier today because we have social networking sites such as Facebook, Twitter, Yahoo groups, and Meetup.com that allow us to come together in ways that were impossible a few decades ago.

WE International offers walk-ins and other spiritual seekers the opportunity to connect, share thoughts and stories, and find community with people who have gone through personal transformation. Most are walk-ins, but some are born-ins interested in learning more about spiritually-transforming experiences. We welcome your comments about how your life changed as a result of merging higher frequencies of spirit into your physical body. By participating in our in-person gatherings, conference calls, and online tele-classes, you may come into a deeper understanding of the nature of your own divine essence and soul's purpose.

Through diligent practice, many ancient mystics have penetrated and transcended the veil of 3-D illusion and found inner sanctum. But, those mystics stayed in their monasteries and convents rather than going back into the marketplace to impart this knowledge to the general population. As walk-ins, we are out there in the marketplace sharing the message of oneness and wholeness. Invariably, we walk-ins find and recognize each other. Our guidance might say, "Why not go to this meeting?" or "Why not email or call so and so?" or "Share your story with this group of people." That is likely how you found this book.

Walk-ins come from a different reality. The walk-in soul is keenly focused on the work it has come to do. Living authentically is very important; therefore, the masks and walls many humans live behind simply do not serve the goals of the walk-in soul. Part of the work that allows you to begin your mission requires letting go of anything that is not serving your authentic self. Otherwise, you may feel stuck indefinitely and never start enjoying the mission that you came here to accomplish. The best way to resolve the natal soul's contracts and energy imprint is through spiritual purification practices such as meditation and prayer in which you surrender to the higher plan for your life. Remember to do RBQT© to support this process.

Your attitude reflects your self-worth, which is molded by the beliefs you have about yourself. The statement, "You are God," upsets a lot of people and many might think you are crazy for saying that. But if we are all connected to and part of the Oneness of the I Am Presence or Source, then we *are* God. We are mini versions (individuations) of the Divine. Most have not lived as such because they have not believed it is possible. People are becoming more sensitive and psychic, but some do not know what to do with these gifts. I encourage you to joyfully use whatever gifts you have, and know that you are supported on your evolutionary path.

Not all of our soul energy can be housed or held in our body as it is configured right now. If we tried to embody all of our soul essence right now, it might severely damage or kill the body. That is why the ascension is a process of restructuring the body and its DNA to contain more light. Be gentle with yourself and allow each day to unfold the beauty that it holds for you personally.

If you have not yet done so, I expect you will soon start to experience the reality of living as a multi-dimensional being. As old patterns and programs are dismantled and higher octave frequencies are embodied, you will begin to have longer periods of bliss and feel the energy of radiant light flowing throughout your body. Now that you are shifting your attitude and response to a more positive vibration, you will not lose focus or get distracted when something upsetting comes along. Living more in the now moment, your emotions will become more stable. Your relationships and business practices will change as you learn to create in higher dimensions. Your prayers and affirmations will begin to manifest more quickly on Earth. Like the saying goes, "As above, so below." It is my prayer that we all flow effortlessly in a stream of ease and well-being as we come to live in unity consciousness.

I would say to all of those who have walked in, "Welcome to Earth. Do your best to stay grounded and not be affected by other people's emotions, thoughts, and feelings. Create a strong personal 18-inch space, do not give away your power, do not absorb energies from others, or take on the chaos of the world. Find your bliss, and do your best to stay in your body. Do not be concerned about what others think. It does not matter if they call you crazy, strange, or weird. Those are just words. What counts is what you know to be true about your multidimensional self. No matter what things look like on the physical plane, know that you are deeply and unconditionally loved by God, Mother Earth, the angels, ascended masters, spirit helpers, galactic beings, and all of creation. I encourage you to set aside fifteen to thirty minutes each day to meditate and hold the thought and feeling that you are loved, supported, and making it just fine in your role on Earth. When you are happy, you are fulfilling your mission."

It is time to come together as one to unify, harmonize, balance, and love one another as we usher in a new Earth. It is time to join hands and create the loving planet we have all dreamed of. This is the shift in consciousness we have talked about and have been preparing for. So, do everything you can to raise your vibration and prepare your physical body to house the new being you are. You no longer have a need for the illnesses you once had or the programming that once ruled your life. We are not the same people we were before. It's time for us to come together and support each other in raising our own personal energy frequencies. Don't be surprised if the people you once hung out with can no longer support you on your mission. As you let go of those relationships, new friends will come along as you reach out to the spiritual community online or in your local area.

It is only natural for people struggling with personal challenges to wonder if they have experienced a walk-in. I invite you to go within and find your own answers that help you explain your life and soul's path. Everyone's core mission is the same: to be unconditional love in motion by living from a compassionate heart.

Regardless of how or when you arrived, I honor your courage to be a spirit on Earth having a human experience during this time of ascension. I pray that those who are about to walk into a mature body have a successful, gentle integration. I pray that those who have been here awhile will witness greater joy in carrying out their mission. I am here as a coach to help you enrich your journey, find your truth, and live on purpose as you strengthen your alignment to the highest aspects of your multidimensional soul.

Bibliography

"Harmonic Convergence." *Wikipedia*. Wikimedia Foundation, 12 Mar. 2013. Web. 10 Jan. 2013.

"Sexual Energy & Creativity." Channel Angels, n.d. Web. 22 Dec. 2012.

Anami, Kim. "Sexual Energy and Creative Genius." *MindBodyGreen*. MindBodyGreen, LLC, 28, Mar. 2012. Web. 22 Feb. 2013

Bright, Susie. "Sexual Energy As Creative Force." *Utne Reader*. Ogden Publications, Inc., Sept,-Oct. 1999. Web. 5 Jan. 2013.

Casey. Email Interview. 15 April 2013.

Cherry, Alexandria K. "Multiple Personality Disorder: Fact or Fiction?" *PersonalityResearch.org*. Rochester Institute of Technology, March 2005. Web. 2 Nov. 2012.

DeLiso, Tom. "The Monad: Your Soul, Your Higher-Self, Your Spirit." *Wisdom's Door*. Wisdomsdoor/Reality Creator Books, n.d. Web. 3 Dec. 2012.

Evans, June. Email Interview. June 2010-Jan. 2013.

Hill, Napoleon. "The Mystery of Sex Transmutation." *Think and Grow Rich*. Meriden, Conn., The Ralston Society, 1938. *Sacred-Texts.com*. Web. 19 Feb. 2013

Kumara, Kenji. Interview on We Are One in Spirit Podcast. 16 Oct. 2012.

Mathison, Carla. "Limbic System." *Instructional Technology Services*. San Diego State University, n.d. Web. 18 Feb. 2013.

Morningstar, Diana. Personal Interview. 26 Mar. 2013.

Pratt, David. "The Monad: One and Many." DavidPratt.com, Feb. 2003. Web. 22, Dec. 2012.

Ranoli. "Contact/About." *Walk-in Evolution*. WE International, n.d. Web. 2 Nov. 2012.

Ranoli. "History." *Walk in Evolution*. WE International, n.d. Web. 2 Nov. 2012.

Remen, Rachel Naomi. Quotable Quote. Goodreads.com. n.d. Web 20 Apr. 2013.

Renee, Lisa. "Ascension Classes." *EnergeticSynthesis.com*. Energetic Synthesis, n.d. Web. 22 Jan. 2013.

Sen. "Channel Your Sexual Energy." *CalmDownMind.com*. Calm Down Mind, 12 Nov. 2011. Web. 2 Jan. 2013.

Williams, Brenda. Personal Interviews. Nov. 2012-Feb. 2013.

About the Author

In November 2012, Yvonne M. Perry the presidency of Walk-in Evolution (WE International), LLC. She immediately set her intention to revive this group of indigo starseeds originally organized by Liz Nelson.

Yvonne holds a Bachelor of Science in Metaphysics from the American Institute of Holistic Theology. In addition to providing spiritual coaching to empaths (HSP) and walk-ins, she is also the author of several books to help people open to a broader understanding of their expression as multidimensional beings on Earth.

Based in Nashville, Tennessee, Yvonne is the founder of We Are One in Spirit and the host of We Are One in Spirit Podcast. She is available as a keynote speaker and workshop leader. Yvonne is also the owner of Writers in the Sky Creative Writing Services, a business she established in 2003 to assist authors in getting their well-written books and articles to the public.

Printed in Great Britain
by Amazon